# Lesbians

# Lesbians
## Where Are We Now?

### Julie Bindel

FORUM

# FORUM

First published in Great Britain by Forum, an imprint of Swift Press 2025

Copyright © Julie Bindel 2025

The right of Julie Bindel to be identified as the Author of this Work has been asserted in accordance with the Copyright, Designs and Patents Act 1988

Typeset by Tetragon, London
Printed and bound in Great Britain by CPI Group (UK) Ltd, Croydon, CR0 4YY

A CIP catalogue record for this book is available from the British Library

We make every effort to make sure our products are safe for the purpose for which they are intended. Our authorised representative in the EU for product safety is Easy Access System Europe, Mustamäe tee 50, 10621 Tallinn, Estonia gpsr.requests@easproject.com

ISBN: 9781800754270
eISBN: 9781800754287

*This book is lovingly dedicated to the late
Lee Lakeman. Lee made a huge, positive difference
to the world she inhabited, and leaves behind a
blueprint for future generations of feminists.*

# Contents

*Note on Terminology*     ix

Introduction     1
    **1** What Does 'Lesbian' Mean to Me?     11
    **2** What's Feminism Got to Do with It? Why Lesbians Are Central to Women's Liberation     43
    **3** Why and How We Are Hated     73
    **4** The Trans Trojan Horse Trots Into Town     97
    **5** Brothers in Arms     135
    **6** Lesbian Activism     161
Epilogue: An Ending and a New Beginning     177

*Notes*     189
*Acknowledgements*     197

# Note on Terminology

I am a feminist and therefore reject the notion that gender is in any way innate. It is the product of patriarchy and amounts to the imposition of sex stereotypes on women and girls.

Until fairly recently, there was a consensus among feminists that gender was a social construct and sex a biological reality. In rejecting the notion that 'femininity' and 'masculinity' are part of our DNA, we were acknowledging that this was an excuse to treat females as a subordinate sex class compared to males.

As a consequence of all this, although I may sometimes (depending on the circumstances) refer to trans-identified individuals by their preferred pronouns and using terms such as 'trans man/woman' (a biological woman and man, respectively), I mostly try to use the correct sex. Today, it is seen as an act of aggression and extreme insensitivity to 'misgender' an individual, but as I say, I consider gender to be a social construct.

I do make exceptions. Occasionally it feels unnecessarily rude to refer to a person as their birth sex, for example someone who acknowledges their own biological sex but has lived as the opposite sex for some time and is not antagonistic about the issue. I'm aware this can be seen as hypocritical, but sometimes it's just good manners to not upset a person when there are no stakes involved, in other words when it's a personal exchange.

But for lesbians in particular I would argue it is hugely important to be realistic about biological sex. We have rejected male bodies and sexuality, and that boundary is crucial to maintain, partly because we are so regularly and often threateningly challenged on this.

# Introduction

When I first came out in 1977, I was full of self-hatred, self-doubt and confusion. And now, almost 50 years later, when I still see lesbians coming under pressure to apologise for their existence, I cannot stay silent. Shutting up has never been my biggest strength; an old school friend, Kate, still talks about the time I entered the school beauty contest as protest candidate Fag-Ash Lil – and won.

There is a new and insidious version of lesbian hatred emerging in the UK. An example: a recent article,[1] one of many covering the now-holy month of Pride, entitled 'Reclaiming lesbian: Why the label ISN'T problematic & the TERFs[2] can't have it'. It was co-written by a lesbian and a man claiming to be a lesbian, Mey Rude, who has worked in lesbian media for a decade. In it, Rude states: 'For me... coming out as a lesbian meant freedom, joy, and self-acceptance, but for many these days it seems to mean policing, transphobia, and division. We're not going to stand for that.' This is a straight man telling *actual* lesbians who are critical of gender ideology that we are less worthy of the word than he is. How did we get here?

The founders of the lesbian and gay liberation movement of the 1960s and 1970s defined themselves as an oppressed minority. Theirs was not a movement for revolutionary social change. But there also existed a movement led by lesbian feminists which demanded the total liberation of *all* women, including the right to sexual self-determination.

In 1981, aged 19, I saw *Town Bloody Hall*, a film of a debate held at the Town Hall Theatre in Manhattan a decade earlier. The film did not have a cinematic release until 1979 – the original director, D. A. Pennebaker, thought the footage unusable, but his wife, the award-winning documentary maker Chris Hegedus, rescued it in the mid-1970s, and the pair edited it together. A feminist group I belonged to got hold of a copy and held a screening as part of a fundraiser to pay for legal advice for one of our number who had been charged with driving a car through the window of a sex shop. In a room above a pub, we watched the film on a cranky projector with awe and amusement as what started out as the apotheosis of liberal, apologetic feminism exploded into a full-blown display of lesbian feminist pride.

The subtitle of *Town Bloody Hall* was 'A Dialogue on Women's Liberation', the implied question being *Is there any need for a feminist movement?* The panel was made up of four high-profile feminist writers, chaired by the notoriously macho Norman Mailer. In his recently published book *The Prisoner of Sex*, Mailer had railed against the new generation of feminist thinkers that included lesbians such as Kate Millett, author of *Sexual Politics*, an account of the subjugation of women in literature and art which included an unflattering reference to Mailer, and which had caused a sensation on its publication a year previously. Panellists

# Introduction

Jacqueline Ceballos, Germaine Greer and Diana Trilling gave various presentations about sexism in literature, while Mailer preened for the cameras.

Then it was Jill Johnston's turn. Johnston was a lesbian feminist activist who wrote for the downtown newspaper the *Village Voice*. As she strode to the podium, it was obvious that she was very different from her heterosexual, liberal co-panellists. Clearly not giving a damn what Norman Mailer thought, she began to speak, and was immediately met with both whoops of joy and shrieks of disapproval. In her patchwork jeans, her face devoid of make-up, she began:

'All women are lesbians, except those who don't know it, naturally. They are but don't know it yet.'

Other highlights from her speech, which ignored the boring conventions of grammar and syntax, included:

'I am a woman and therefore a lesbian, I am a woman who is a lesbian because I am a woman, and a woman who loves herself naturally, who is other women is a lesbian. A woman who loves women loves herself. Naturally, this is the case. A woman is herself, is all woman, is a natural born lesbian. So we don't mind using the name like any name it is quite meaningless. It means naturally, I am a woman and whatever I am we are, we affirm being what we are...

'There is in every perfect love a law to be accomplished, too, that the lover should resemble the beloved and be the same, and the greater is the likeness, the brighter will the rapture flame. To be equal we have to become who we really are, and women, we will never be equal women until we love one another, women.

'I want men... to adore me as a lesborated woman.

'Until all women are lesbians, there will be no true political revolution.'

When she ran over her allotted time, Mailer, looking as though his scrotum had shrunk all the way up into his abdomen, started to tell her, rather aggressively, that she had to stop. At that point, Johnston's girlfriend and another woman leapt up on the stage, and the three women began kissing and rolling around on the floor. The audience was gasping with a combination of horror and delight, as Johnston ignored pleas from Mailer to 'be a lady'. As the three of them cavorted, he sneered, 'It's great that you pay 25 bucks to see three dirty overalls on the floor, when you can see lots of cock and cunt for four bucks just down the street.' A woman in the audience shouted, 'What's wrong with you, Mailer, have you found a woman you can't fuck?', to which he replied, 'Hey cunty, I've been threatened all my life, take it easy.'

What happened on stage between Johnston and the two other lesbians had a huge impact on everyone who saw it. It has been described as the very first public display of lesbianism that was totally irreverent and all about celebratory fun.

In sharp contrast to Greer, who was sporting a – quickly discarded – fur wrap, slinky sleeveless black dress, sultry eye make-up and a classic early seventies shag haircut, talking a hard feminist line while flirting with Mailer and playing to the men in the audience, Johnston exuded pride, irreverence and a complete disdain for male approval. The other women on the panel, selected for their intellectual rigour and ability to articulate unpopular feminist views challenging male supremacy, paled into insignificance next to Johnston's magnificent defiance. As her widow Ingrid Nyeboe told me, 'Jill gave us permission to be who we are. Without feeling bad about it, without thinking that something was wrong with us. And as she always said, we were the most radical, we were the most revolutionary.' That moment in *Town Bloody Hall* was full of joy and rebellion. And the resulting outrage at unapologetic lesbian existence being celebrated in a public sphere told its own story.

It is important to understand the context in which Johnston was operating. Betty Friedan, author of *The Feminine Mystique*, a book sometimes credited as the catalyst for second-wave feminism, and co-founder and first president of the National Organization for Women (NOW), was in the audience at the *Town Bloody Hall* debate. The previous year, she had referred to lesbians in NOW who wanted to come out of the closet and champion their cause as 'the lavender menace'. She was convinced that lesbians were giving the women's movement a bad name and even attempted to purge them from the organisation. Later that same year, Kate Millett was on a panel at an event at Columbia University. In attendance was a woman from the group called the radicalesbians, set up to oppose the bigotry of Friedan's comments and her subsequent actions. This woman stood up and asked Millett why she had not yet come out as a lesbian – implying that, by remaining in the closet, Millett had handed ammunition to Friedan.

Two weeks later, *Time* magazine, which had featured Millett on its front cover and lauded *Sexual Politics* as 'groundbreaking', referred to her as a 'bisexual' whose sexuality would fragment the Women's Liberation Movement, thus lending credibility to Friedan and her allies who were unhappy about the growing prominence of lesbians. A rally was organised in support of

Millett, and the attendees, including Friedan, were asked to wear a lavender armband in solidarity. One story goes that Friedan threw hers to the floor and stamped on it. It's difficult to believe a so-called feminist would treat lesbians in that way now, with insults and attempts at censorship. But the question remains: where are today's lesbian heroes, our very own Jill Johnstons?

Received wisdom has it that we are fully integrated into society and enjoy full legal equality – particularly if we live in the global north. But have we really progressed beyond that, to the point of true liberation from prejudice, discrimination and anti-lesbian tropes?

I was constantly told as a young lesbian that lesbianism was 'unnatural' and that it was impossible for two women to have sex without a man. The bad old days indeed. But then in 2021, Nancy Kelley, former CEO of Stonewall, described as bigots lesbians who exclude 'trans women', i.e. men who say they are women, from our dating pool, which equally translates into pressure to have sex with men. (According to Kelley, lesbians who are 'trans exclusionary' are akin to 'sexual racists'.)[3]

As I write, it is 51 years since the publication of Johnston's book, *Lesbian Nation: The Feminist Solution*, a key feminist text in which she set out her revolutionary and joyful vision of radical lesbian feminism. And 20 years ago I would have stated, confidently and unequivocally, that lesbians were never going back in the closet – that there had been a cultural revolution when it came to lesbian lives. But today, I believe that lesbians are facing a tidal wave of misogyny, and a backlash that threatens to return us to a life on the margins and in the shadows. In this book I describe this threat to lesbian existence and propose

## Introduction

ways for us to clear these hurdles and get us back on the path to true liberation.

We all need to face up to the fact that women's and lesbian liberation cannot exist without each other. The past 20 years have seen a sea change in sexual politics with the emergence of the so-called 'gender wars'. There are several reasons why I have spoken out against gender ideology – in an infamous newspaper article in 2004, entitled 'Gender Benders, Beware', in which I argued that transsexuality is nothing but the promotion of sexist stereotypes,[4] as well as around the kitchen table and at public events. One is the continuing prevalence of male violence against all women and girls, irrespective of how they 'identify', recently described by the UK National Police Chiefs' Council as 'a national emergency'.[5] Another is how difficult it is now for lesbians to find women-only spaces where we can meet, socialise and organise. And yet another is that I see more and more women who refuse to bow to the demands of gender ideologues hounded out of jobs, thrown off college courses and frozen out of friendship networks. I cannot help but note that many of those most targeted are lesbians. Our demands for autonomy are met with particularly vicious hatred and misogyny from trans activists. They come after us that bit harder. Unless we agree to include men in our spaces, we are denounced as bigots and even taken to court. We are denied our place on Pride marches if we are deemed 'trans exclusionary'. We are told that our right to use the word 'lesbian' depends on our accepting that some women have penises.

For this book, I have interviewed lesbians of all ages in countries around the world and uncovered fascinating historical and contemporary stories that show how lesbians have always, *always* resisted male dominance. By our very existence, we present a threat to the patriarchy. And as such, we are key to the achievement of genuine liberation for all women.

This all crystallised for me in 2020. Lesbians were being kicked off Pride marches; black, working-class lesbian barrister Allison Bailey was subjected to a formal investigation by her chambers for a tweet welcoming the formation of the LGB Alliance; Nancy Kelley said that it is 'exclusionary' for lesbians to refuse to date men who say they are women. It was then that I had the idea of setting up a new organisation aimed at improving the wellbeing of same-sex-attracted females. I asked Kathleen Stock, a philosophy professor and lesbian feminist who was being subjected to harassment at her university, Sussex, because of her views on sex and gender, to be my collaborator. During the Covid lockdown, Kathleen and I spent countless hours talking about the vilification of lesbians who dared to speak out against gender ideology and thought it important to uphold the law on single-sex spaces and services. We were both aware of the erasure of lesbians as a separate category within the 'queer' rainbow and wanted to do something to put lesbians back on the map. Both Kathleen and I also wanted to challenge the damaging, defamatory lies that were being told about us and the slurs that were being hurled at us.

When Kathleen's book *Material Girls: Why Reality Matters for Feminism* was published in May 2021, trans activists upped the ante, and, following the most horrendous, frightening harassment by students, who received the tacit support of some of her colleagues, Kathleen resigned her post. We now had time to

## Introduction

make our ideas a reality, and The Lesbian Project was formally founded in March 2023. One of our first initiatives was a weekly podcast where Kathleen and I, and sometimes special guests, talk about all things lesbian, have a laugh, and get down to some serious business. It has quickly established itself as a fixture for thousands of listeners around the world.

I have been lucky in life: since finding feminism and meeting other lesbians at a fairly young age, I've been completely content with my sexuality. I have been in an extremely happy and fulfilling relationship since I was 25. Having travelled the world investigating crimes against women, in particular those involving male violence, I have met many lesbians who have been severely punished both for being who they are and for rejecting men sexually and emotionally. I am well aware that there are many lesbians, including in the UK, whose lives are much more difficult than anything I could now imagine for myself.

Have lesbians always been hated, looked upon with suspicion and derision, and considered less than 'real' women? Yes. But now is the time to take what is ours – the freedom and liberation we deluded ourselves into believing we had already won.

This book is neither a personal memoir nor a history lesson on lesbians through the ages. It will, I hope, bring some clarity to an extremely contested sexual identity; we are in new territory, with the word 'lesbian' up for grabs, even as it is being rejected by lesbians, particularly the young. But the attack on lesbians is the sharp end of the attack on women. The way lesbians are treated is a yardstick for society's misogyny. If we are free, then all women are free.

# 1

# What Does 'Lesbian' Mean to Me?

While all identities and sexualities are welcome at La Cam, [the owners] were intentional in labelling the bar 'lesbian', as both a reclamation and a celebration. While some people tend to think lesbian means cis women who love other cis women, for Loveless and Solis it is 'open to whoever wants to claim it'... They are also happy with Flinta (female, lesbian, intersex, nonbinary, trans and agender)... thanks to its inclusive overtones.

La Camionera: this lesbian bar in Hackney is London's new hotspot', Hattie Collins, *The Times*, 8 June 2024

If I didn't define myself, I would be crunched into other people's fantasies for me and eaten alive.

From a 1982 address given by Audre Lorde as part of the Celebration of Malcolm X Weekend at Harvard University

In 1982, I was 20 and living in Leeds with a job on a Youth Opportunities Programme at a National Health Service project. My manager there, Lesley, was an out lesbian and proud feminist, which is what bonded us, despite significant differences in age (she was about fifteen years older than me), class background and social status. She asked me to help her set up a Lesbian Line for the region, a helpline for lesbians equivalent to the Gay Switchboard.

Having no premises, we asked the men who ran the Gay Switchboard if we could use theirs every Tuesday between 7 and 9pm. Lesley explained to them why this was necessary: even though they advertised their service as being open to both men and women, we knew that lesbians would not want to speak to gay men about their lives, no matter how warm and friendly they were. The gay men resisted this argument, telling us that there was no such thing as a 'typical lesbian'; the women calling the helpline would come from every walk of life, and could have as much in common with gay men as with other lesbians. We explained that there are certain issues that bind lesbians together, and that only we could really understand one another. We asked them if they thought the gay men would find it reassuring to speak to a lesbian on the switchboard about some of their problems. They looked bewildered – but they gave us a set of keys.

Every Tuesday evening from then on, whoever was on shift would sit in a dingy basement for two hours to take calls from women of all ages and circumstances. To raise funds for the line, and to give callers desperate to meet other lesbians a place to go, we persuaded the landlord of a pub called the Dock Green to let us use his (otherwise empty) upstairs bar to host a fortnightly women-only disco. Given how much the Leeds lesbians drank, it was a very good business move on his part.

Word got around, and local lesbians were soon joined by those from neighbouring towns and cities – Todmorden, Hebden

## What Does 'Lesbian' Mean to Me?

Bridge and Manchester – turning up every two weeks to talk, dance, plot and connect. I'd find myself in conversations with self-described 'gay women' who would tell me why they were voting Tory as I sat there aghast. There were women who would spend all evening talking about who they fancied, and explaining that when a butch takes a femme out, she never allows her to pay. I was appalled: to me it sounded just the same as staying at home on my housing estate and marrying a local boy. Except it wasn't – because it was being said by another woman.

When running Lesbian Line, the importance of a specific lesbian-only support network became clear to me through the women who needed our help. Carrie first called us in great distress because her violent ex-husband was applying for full custody of their little boy. She had felt she had to hide the fact that she was now in a relationship with a woman, but had eventually told her parents and a few close friends. She then turned up at the Dock Green, distraught, after the court granted full custody of her child to his father. She was worried both that she would never see her son again and that his father would abuse and neglect him. She said something I have never forgotten: 'He only wants him to punish me.' Among the Dock Green regulars was a solicitor who had dealt with similar terrible cases in the family court, who on hearing the story sat down beside Carrie, offering both reassurance and immediate advice. Members of a feminist group supporting lesbian mothers came over to speak to her. The bar dykes (working-class lesbians, often butch identified) bought her a drink, and one of them talked her into a couple of games of pool. When I next saw Carrie, a few months later, she told me that there was a hearing in a week's time, and that she was hoping to regain custody of her child. 'I've joined the club,' she said bashfully. 'I'm one of you now.' She meant, of course, that she had become a feminist.

On another occasion, a young woman, Mary, who was probably still in her teens, turned up and told the women working the door that she couldn't afford the entrance fee, but please could we let her in because she desperately needed to talk to her friends. She explained that a neighbour had spotted her kissing a girl and told her parents. They threw her out because their religious beliefs were the kind that didn't hold with same-sex attraction, and they didn't want her influencing her younger sister. It turned out that in reality she had no friends at the disco, but she had known that we would look after her. Between us – the bar dykes (again), the older feminists and everyone else – we found her a place to stay, gave her some money and took her for a curry. We had all, to some extent, been through what she had: every single one of us had at some point faced rejection, homelessness, self-exclusion or stigmatisation. The next time I saw Mary was at a demonstration organised by Women Against Violence Against Women, a protest group I was involved in, outside a new strip club on its opening night. Most of us were lesbians. There was a fairly big crowd, and there was Mary with her new girlfriend. She was living in a squat with a lesbian collective and having a great time.

Both Carrie and Mary had, through our work on the Lesbian Line, discovered what we all knew: our only way forward was through feminist support, solidarity and connections.

◆

# What Does 'Lesbian' Mean to Me?

## How I define a lesbian

My definition of a lesbian is a woman (i.e. female) who is sexually attracted to other women (i.e. other females). It is not a requirement to be sexually active or in a relationship with another woman to claim that identity of 'lesbian'; you don't stop being a lesbian because your relationship ends, and there are women who have never had a sexual encounter or relationship who nevertheless use this term to describe themselves. As far as I am concerned, the only requirement for a woman to define herself as a lesbian is that she prioritises other women in her personal life and does not seek out and consensually engage in sexual relationships with men. I recognise of course that many lesbians are in relationships with men because they have not yet come out, for whatever reason. And there are others who have chosen to remain in a relationship that does not sexually or emotionally fulfil them for the sake of financial security, or a desire for family unity. And there are others still who are coerced into heterosexual lives because the alternative is total rejection by family and other punitive consequences. Some women may well have lesbian tendencies, feelings or aspirations, but the element of choice in being an out lesbian is crucial to lesbian feminism. If you could choose to be a lesbian, would you willingly make that choice?

There are endless discussions around lesbian sexuality. Are babies born with a sexual orientation that emerges around the time of puberty, or is the way our sexuality evolves more complicated than that? Is there such a thing as a 'gay gene', or does sexual attraction and orientation develop through a nexus of circumstances, opportunity and other factors not connected to our genes or DNA? Is there a bisexual gene? Is everyone who doesn't conform to the norm some type of rebel or, as some now would have it, 'queer'? To what extent is lesbianism a political identity?

In my experience, being a lesbian is not *just* about sexual orientation; it is about belonging to a community in which women prioritise each other, where there is a sense of political solidarity with other women, and *particularly* with other lesbians. As the only sexual orientation that excludes men, we are a danger to the established social and political order, and as I pointed out earlier, we are the first group to be targeted in the backlash against feminism.

## My beginnings

I was raised by loving parents in Darlington in the north-east of England. We lived on a council estate, and I attended a failing comprehensive school. When I was 12, I developed a crush on a school friend. It wasn't about sex – I was too young for that; it was more of a puppy-love sort of thing. I wanted her to be my friend. I thought everything about her was wonderful. She was less interested in me than I was in her, which broke my heart a bit.

I was never interested in boys, and the ones at my school – most of them horrible bullies – informed me that I was a lesbian before I even knew what a lesbian was. There were only two types of girls at my school – 'slags' and 'lezzers'. It was the boys who decided who fell into which category. To be a slag, you had to have had sex (or it had to be rumoured that you had), whether consensual or not, with at least one boy. All you had to do to be a lezzer was avoid having sex with boys and show no interest in them at all.

At 15, I fell madly in love with a schoolmate called Josie – we were also both Saturday girls at a hair salon in town. This time it was reciprocated, and we spent some blissful times together. But it was too hard for us not to be found out. There was no way we could be open as lesbians. We could not even use the word – which was repulsive even to us. We drifted apart, and I started hanging out with David, a gay boy from the salon, who took me to my first gay club.

The clientele of Rockshots in Newcastle was largely made up of male go-go dancers and amazing butch women. I loved it, and felt at home there. There were also drag queens, transvestites and cross-dressing women, as well as older lesbians and gay men who had grown up in much harder times. Every night, as we left, groups of thuggish men would shout obscenities at us – presumably their idea of a fun post-closing-time leisure activity. The gay men, including the drag queens, would protect us women, and they often got a pasting for it. One time, I found myself surrounded by a gang of five or six of these bullies, and honestly feared for my life. Once I had been rescued, we went to the local greasy spoon to calm down and sober up, but the owner refused to serve us, calling us dirty perverts as he chucked us out.

When I left school, I had no qualifications and no idea what I was going to do with my life. I knew that I had to get out of Darlington, and began writing to lesbians who'd placed ads in the 'Seeking Friends' section of *Gay News*. Eventually, I made contact with a handful of young women in nearby towns and cities and met Diane, a young woman who had recently escaped a relationship with a violent man. Diane was the daughter of an Italian mother and a black (heritage unknown) father and had been adopted at the age of four by a white Catholic couple from Selby, North Yorkshire. She had suffered years of racist abuse at the hands of her schoolmates in the almost all-white town, and had been sexually abused by her adoptive grandfather. Her horrific childhood and adolescence took its toll on her mental health and at 17, when she came out as a lesbian, her adoptive parents kicked her out. Finding herself homeless and in a very vulnerable state, Diane ended up living with the father of a school friend. Four years later, still in a controlling and violent relationship with this man, Diane answered my letter to *Gay News*.

At 21, Diane was four years older than me, and was doing an apprenticeship at a high-end hair salon in Leeds. The commute from York, where she was living, and her dire situation with her friend's horrible father were wearing her down. Having begun a relationship, we both decided to move to Leeds: this proved to be a major turning point in my life. Although our relationship ended after four years, we stayed close, and more than 40 years later we remain in each other's lives, like family.

## Finding feminism, understanding lesbians

Diane and I moved together into the YMCA hostel in Headingley, close to the university. Over the road was the Corner Bookshop, a leftist, 'alternative' hangout. On its noticeboard, I spotted a poster advertising something called a consciousness-raising group, which I eventually worked out was a place for women to discuss issues normally off limits: childhood sexual abuse, domestic violence, rape and sexual assault. I went along to a meeting, where something called 'female sexuality and pleasure' was on the agenda. Heterosexual feminists dominated the conversation, speaking very openly about the lack of sexual excitement in their relationships with men. 'My husband wouldn't be able to tell a clitoris from an elbow', said one. The lesbians, on the other hand, when they got to speak, talked about how wonderful it was to be intimate with other women. All my life I had been told that being a lesbian meant something was wrong with me; suddenly it was being described as something positive – even wonderful.

Rockshots aside, my only forays into lesbian culture had been in the working-class bars of Newcastle. I would turn up, terrified of being kidnapped by the predatory butch lesbians I had heard so much about. In fact, the first young woman who ever approached me and asked me to dance was dressed as a Bay City Roller.[1] I was yet to meet the feminists who would educate me and reassure me that I was not a freak or a pervert or 'really a boy'. The lesbians I knew in those days came in two main varieties: there were the bar dykes I have already described – quite 'traditional' lesbians who generally organised themselves into butch and femme identities, and socialised in hired rooms above mainstream pubs, away from 'normal' people. They were almost all working class, veterans of lesbian culture. Many had been in the armed forces, which was a 'respectable' way of avoiding 'compulsory heterosexuality' (a phrase coined in 1980 by the US feminist author and poet Adrienne Rich),[2] marriage and children.

Then there were the feminist lesbians, mostly middle class, who were very political about their sexuality. Knowing heterosexuality to be bad for women under patriarchy, these lesbians saw their sexual orientation as liberating and wholly positive. They were comrades-in-arms, as well as lovers.

I soon threw in my lot with the feminist lesbians, though not without some angst. I was solidly working class, and well out of my comfort zone having dinner with them, enduring undercooked baked potato with vegan spread, and chewy aubergine – a vegetable I had never previously encountered. But for all that, those lesbians were beyond inspirational for me. They taught me how to feel pride in myself, and anger about male violence towards and dominance over women. They rejected sex stereotypes and were critical of butch and femme role-play while offering support and friendship to women embedded in that culture. I came to learn that lesbians were hated because women were hated, and that rejecting men sexually was both very dangerous and an exhilarating feminist act. I started to see that if we lesbians could be proud of our identity, neither seeking to hide it nor wishing for a magic pill that could change it, then we would – inevitably – be leading a revolution. This didn't mean heterosexual women couldn't be feminists – the majority of the feminist activists I knew were indeed straight. But we did feel they should recognise that lesbians were at the vanguard of the feminist movement, and acknowledge the contradiction in their own lives – as some of them did.

## What Does 'Lesbian' Mean to Me?

# Born this way?

Then as now, some non-feminist lesbians were hugely offended by the idea that lesbians – either by default, or explicitly and proudly – could be a threat to patriarchy or describe lesbianism as something political. They were so wedded to the notion that lesbians were 'born this way' that they were horrified by the idea that some women might be able to join the club in later life. Many of them thought that claiming lesbianism as a matter of genetic programming would afford them some kind of protection from discrimination. All had faced prejudice; many had been kicked out of their families, communities and jobs, and they believed that 'innateness' could serve as a kind of defence, a reason for their difference. Some also thought it offered protection against being 'converted' by religious figures or psychiatrists. These ideas persist today.

The late 1970s and early 1980s was an exciting time for the Women's Liberation Movement. The Greenham Common Women's Peace Camp, set up in September 1981 at an RAF base in Berkshire as a protest against its use as a storage facility for cruise missiles from the US, came to be a hive of lesbian activism. A number of heterosexual women, often married with children, found themselves so passionately committed to challenging the US military base on their home turf that they left home to join the camp, often staying for weeks on end, some never going back. After a few pints down the Dog and Duck, with the excitement of political protest and sisterly solidarity filling the air, some of these women ended up getting more involved than they might initially have planned.

What do we say about a woman like this? The one who realises there is no going back to her husband – or to heterosexuality in general? Was *she* born this way? Or was it that up until that point she had been denied the possibility of exploring her own sexual desire and had, like many women, been walking through life in a fugue state? Should we expend time and energy on arguing about whether or not she had always been a lesbian? What does it matter?

Feminists tend not to buy the 'born this way' argument because for them, sexual liberation and identity are about having a free and open choice, as opposed to being railroaded into Rich's 'compulsory heterosexuality'. Rich, a feminist author and poet who came out later in life after having children and after the death of her husband, described heterosexuality as 'something that has had to be imposed, managed, organised, propagandised, and maintained by force', and claimed that 'women have been convinced that marriage and sexual orientation toward men are inevitable – even if unsatisfying or oppressive – components of their lives.' For many of the feminists who felt trapped in heterosexual relationships, this was a liberatory moment.

Rich's groundbreaking work was born of the phrase 'the personal is political', a slogan used by feminists at the time to describe the ways in which personal experiences are connected to structural issues in society. Rich challenged heterosexual women to think consciously about their place in the world, and also to understand how life was for lesbians. She defined lesbianism as including 'a range – through each woman's life and throughout history – of women-identified experience, not simply the fact that a woman has had or consciously desired genital sexual experience with another woman'.

'Compulsory heterosexuality' is very much still with us today. It is clothing for three-year-old girls that says 'So many boys, so little time', or screams 'Biggest flirt' in pink glitter. It is women being expected to have relationships with men, from girlhood to death. It is women being vilified or viewed with suspicion and considered inferior unless they marry (a man) by the time they're in their thirties and preferably have children with him. It is feeling shamed (or ashamed) for preferring women to men as romantic and sexual partners. It is being considered odd and an outsider by female friends and colleagues for not having feelings for men. It is being embarrassed (and maybe even humiliated or bullied) for saying that this isn't something you want. It is mothers and fathers telling their daughters that 'the right man' will come along. It is being a disappointment and wanting desperately to fit in, and ending up dating Barry down the road because he's there, and he's interested. We all know and understand it, even if we haven't consciously named it. Compulsory heterosexuality is all of these things and more, the sea we all swim in.

In 1979, the Leeds Revolutionary Feminist Group published a pamphlet entitled *Political Lesbianism: The Case Against Heterosexuality*. In 1981, it was reprinted in a booklet under the title *Love Your Enemy? The Debate Between Heterosexual Feminism and Political Lesbianism*. The authors of the pamphlet argued that women should reject men and become lesbians. The republication highlighted some of the responses to the argument.

The fundamental difference between Rich's views and those of the Leeds Revolutionary Feminist Group is that Rich was exploring the possibilities of women's sexual and romantic/emotional attraction to other women, *if and when* unhindered and blocked by external anti-lesbian forces leading to stigma and other dire consequences for women. As the title makes clear, she views heterosexual desire and coupling as a compulsory state of affairs *under patriarchy*. If women had true freedom and sexual autonomy, more of them would opt for sex and relationships with other females.

The Leeds paper, on the other hand, was a provocative challenge to heterosexual feminists to give up men and to take up lesbianism for the cause. 'We were trying to challenge the excuses used by some heterosexual feminists as to why they lived with Nigel or John,' one of the authors, Tina Crockett, told me back in 2009. 'They said, "Oh, but my man is OK," as a way of refusing to look at the fact that some men really do hate women.' The Leeds paper clearly blamed women for colluding with the patriarchy by having relationships with men. Rich took a more positive and optimistic view, writing: 'I continue to think that heterosexual feminists will draw political strength for change from taking a critical stance toward the ideology which demands heterosexuality, and that lesbians cannot assume that we are untouched by that ideology and the institutions founded upon it.'

Whereas the Leeds political lesbians appeared to hold feminists responsible for not only colluding in their own oppression, but also for betraying other women, Rich was concerned to explain how heterosexuality is imposed upon all women and girls under patriarchy, and therefore women cannot freely choose their sexual orientation. How, asked Rich, do we know if most women are innately heterosexual, when, under patriarchy, we don't have a free and open choice? Women are socialised into heterosexuality, and severely punished for rejecting it. It was not an argument against heterosexuality, or against heterosexual sex, but a clear-minded analysis of how patriarchy works. Rich's theory complemented the fascinating research by feminism's only sexologist, Shere Hite, who had asked the question that had long been ignored or wilfully misrepresented by her male counterparts.

## Hite's lesbian bombshell

I interviewed Hite in 2011,[3] and again in 2014. No male sexologist then (or since) has bothered to address the questions Hite, who died in 2020, raised in her research. Published in 1976 as *The Hite Report: A Nationwide Study of Female Sexuality*, it was based on responses from 3,500 women to questionnaires about their experiences of sex and pleasure. Women between the ages of 14 and 78 answered questions about orgasms, masturbation and their sexual desires, questions that most women could not have asked of even their best friends. By 2000, when more than 20 million copies had been sold, Hite had updated the research.

Two-thirds of Hite's UK respondents claimed that their male partners were ill-informed about women's bodies when they met, and needed to be 'taught'. Many of the heterosexual female respondents were sexually dissatisfied by men: 8 per cent said they preferred sex with women. An additional 9 per cent either identified as bisexual or reported having sexual experiences with both men and women. Hite noted that 'one of the most striking points about the answers received to the other questions was how frequently, *even when it was not specifically asked*, women brought up the fact that they might be interested in having sexual relations with another woman. The following lines are from some of the study's respondents, as quoted in the section of *The Hite Report* entitled 'Lesbianism'.

'I've slept with about 20 men and one woman. I found the woman much better,' said one lesbian respondent.

'No woman has ever asked me *Didja come?* They knew,' said another.

The book's message to men was: women don't need you. Inevitably, Hite was insulted and derided as a man-hater.

Women can, understandably, be very defensive about their sexual desires, and of course some might have no romantic or sexual interest in women at all. I'm not suggesting that every single woman is a latent lesbian. Some of this defensiveness might mask a different reality, which is that a significant minority, possibly even the majority of women, have at some stage in their life experienced a crush on another girl or woman. But perhaps some women are simply not willing to consider the possibility that this attraction could exist for them, because there is far too much at stake to start questioning their choices.

## 'Would you prefer to be "normal"?'

It was not my choice to come out at school, but by the time I was 15, and all the other girls were either dating boys or showing an interest in them, it became obvious I was different. I had a major crush on a girl in my class, and, although I tried not to make it obvious, rumours began to circulate. One day, a particularly nasty bully decided to corner me near the canteen, and asked me what is was like to 'ride another girl'. I blurted out that I was gay (my memory is fuzzy here, but no way would I have used the word lesbian). My fate was sealed: from that day forward, I was a 'dirty lezzer', at least according to the school nasties.

But not everyone was horrible. Some were merely curious or fascinated. I was regularly asked, 'If there were a pill that would make you normal, would you take it?' Partly because it was hard to be different, I would reply, 'Of course!' But that wasn't the only reason for my answer. I had absorbed the idea that not only was I born this way, I was faulty. I believed that something must have gone wrong in my mother's womb, or happened to me when I was very young, that turned me into a lesbian. It was only after hearing the lesbian feminists I met in Leeds talk about how proud they were of their sexual identity as lesbians, how much better the sex was between women, how much freer and more liberating their lives were without men, that I stopped feeling like a weirdo and an outsider and began to feel instead that I belonged to a wonderful society of fabulous women.

There was no suggestion from my Leeds friends that heterosexual women should identify as lesbian on principle; the conversation was about laying bare the truth about heterosexuality for women under patriarchy. Disgruntled, unhappy straight feminists would say things to me like, 'You are lucky being a lesbian, I wish I was, but I just don't fancy women.' I would feel a little offended by this; the implication was that I was a completely different species from them – that, difficult as it was, their sexuality was nonetheless 'normal'. I didn't care one way or the other whether they were attracted to women, but I had my suspicions that, as unhappy with men as they were, they might one day find themselves tempted to break out of their heterosexual straitjackets. It was the lesbians in the group who held out the possibility of true liberation for women, and offered a glimpse of what it would look like.

The idea that if the many barriers and prejudices about lesbianism were broken down, and women had real sexual freedom, many more would act on (or even admit to) a sexual attraction to other women made sense to me. I could imagine having gone along with what was expected of me – marrying a local boy, having children – and finding myself trapped. I would have been one of those women, completely invisible to the lesbian or gay community, who felt compelled to stay in the closet, becoming more entrenched within my heterosexual identity, pushing aside any feelings I might have for other women. I thought I would likely have stayed that way for the rest of my life.

My understanding of lesbianism and female sexuality as a political issue was growing all the time. I was learning about the institution of patriarchy and how it is upheld by heterosexuality, about how women living in conventional nuclear families had less power and a lower status than their male partners, that rape in marriage was then entirely legal, and that hardly any men were ever prosecuted for domestic violence. I grew to see that women rejecting all this and coming out as lesbians was a huge 'fuck you' to the patriarchy and the established order. Resisting heterosexuality was a revolutionary act. If we were out and proud, the question of 'born this way' became irrelevant. What we were doing was not apologising, not wishing to be anything else: we were proud and happy to be lesbians.

## The lesbian continuum

Today, increasing numbers of apparently straight women are questioning their sexual identities, with some perceiving their sexuality as increasingly fluid. According to both Office for National Statistics (ONS) data and a 2023 study by the University of Essex, women are far more likely than men to describe themselves as bisexual, and more prone to changing their minds about their sexuality during their twenties.[4] Instead of declaring themselves either heterosexual or lesbian, many women define themselves more loosely. Perhaps this shift is partly to do with the growing numbers of women in the public eye disclosing that they have, over the years, experienced attraction to both men and women.

Predictably, some – not all – men are put out by this, possibly considering it an abandonment of the 'natural order'. For those who measure masculinity against women's dependency and sexual acquiescence, the apparent slide into sexual flexibility among women compromises their own sense of identity, making them fear they are no longer central to women's lives.

Some lesbians, too, are offended by the concept of a 'fluid' sexuality. These are the women who refer to themselves as 'gold star' lesbians, meaning they have never had sex with a man; they are the 'born this ways' who believe that women who experiment are no more than 'tourists', frivolously toying with the emotions of others for their own sexual gratification. I am not unsympathetic; I understand that women who have fought for the right to be in a same-sex relationship and suffered abuse and violence for exercising that right do not see lesbian identity as a vehicle for a fun night out before a return to the safe space of straightness. But what is the point of rigid ideological purity? Do these women want to be seen as martyrs? As special? The 'gold star' women argue that because some prominent lesbian feminist activists were not forced to marry men (though some women still are, and pretty much every woman used to be), others should be doomed to a life of heterosexuality, with their only options being to accept themselves as heterosexual, or call themselves bisexual. This argument seems another form of compulsory heterosexuality – coming from lesbians! It is an attempt to force or shame these women into accepting that they're attracted to men when they are not. But lesbianism is not a special, elitist club to which only a certain kind of lesbian will be admitted. In an essay about her lesbianism awakening, the Australian feminist writer and academic Renate Klein explained, 'I defined myself as a lesbian radical feminist. The relationships kept coming... and going... bringing the most radiant joy and depth of sadness, but one thing was sure: all my lovers were the most interesting artsy and bookish types and all were of course feminists. Never a dull moment in our lives. Such a good change from my rather boring relationships with men. I never looked back: men were my past, women my future.'[5]

The views of 'gold star' lesbians on this subject are not far off those of certain men, for example Menelaos Apostolou, currently a professor in Humanities and Social Sciences at the University of Nicosia in Cyprus. The argument in his latest book, *The*

## What Does 'Lesbian' Mean to Me?

*Evolution of Same-Sex Attraction*, based on a 2017 study for which not a single lesbian was interviewed, is that men are 'sexually excited' by the idea of their partner having a same-sex attraction, and that lesbians exist in order to cater to this. Speaking over Zoom, Apostolou explained to me that because marriage was until relatively recently compulsory, and homosexuality illegal, sometimes on pain of death, 'during most of human evolution, same-sex attraction wouldn't impair reproductive effort'. He added that for some women, there are benefits to being a lesbian. 'All research indicates... that there is a genetic basis to [same-sex attraction],' he claims. This man is a professor at a high-ranking university whose work is published in prestigious peer-reviewed journals, and he believes that lesbians have not become obsolete, despite indulging only in non-reproductive sexual behaviour, only because some men get off on their girlfriends having sex with other women. His anti-scientific and nonsensical conclusions are based on stereotypes, myths and male entitlement. (If this sounds familiar, it is, of course, the same kind of thinking that informs gender ideology, which we will come to later.)

I don't want to live in a world where people feel they must hang on to the labels they adopted or were given early on – especially when those labels leave them unhappy or unfulfilled. As many of the Greenham women illustrate, in the course of campaigning for social change women have also dramatically changed their own lives. Similarly, during the long and bitter miners' strike of 1984–85, the miners' wives embraced a women-oriented political culture not unlike that at the heart of the Greenham peace camp, and sometimes alongside it discovered a new sexual identity for themselves. Women who signed up for some of the inspirational early Women's Studies courses, hoping perhaps to make small changes to the division of labour at home, ended up wanting completely different lives, uncluttered by and independent of men. Joan Scanlon is a lesbian feminist who, among many other things, taught at the first week-long Open University Women's Studies summer school in 1987. The original course was called 'The Changing Experience of Women' and focused on the material reality of women's lives, including violence against women. It ran for over a decade, organised and taught by academics, most of whom were also grassroots feminists. 'There were those who thought the course was a soft option, and those who were actively looking for feminism,' recalls Scanlon. 'Above all, it was accessible. This very diverse group of women would rock up for the week. You had coupons for food, you didn't do any cooking, you didn't do any washing, you didn't do any housework. And for a lot of the women who came to that course, it was the first time they'd been away without their kids. And by the end of the week, some of them had fallen in love with another woman and were planning to leave their male partners – it was gobsmacking.' The summer school became a legendary event. I myself have met a woman who when she signed up for the course was heterosexual, married, and somewhat bored with her husband. By the time I talked to her, she had left her husband and was dating a woman she had met through the friends she made there. They are still together.

Scanlon witnessed similar scenarios countless times. Extraordinary changes could happen when women were given the space to discuss and debate issues in their lives and make sense of them within a feminist framework. 'It might sound like an exaggeration, but in the course of one week, women underwent extraordinary revolutions in their lives. There were quite a few lesbian feminists teaching on it, who always held a session at the very beginning of the week called, after Adrienne Rich, "Compulsory Heterosexuality and Lesbian Existence". The idea was to make sure that any lesbians in the group got to meet each other early on, so they didn't feel isolated during the week. But also, I think, to get the issue of lesbianism out there in the open.' The combination of discussing feminist theory and the opportunity simply to be among other women, including lesbians, thinking, talking, drinking into the night, was, as at Greenham, enough for some previously pretty conventional women to branch out. Scanlon herself could barely believe what was happening. 'I don't know what percentage we're talking about, but it was a phenomenon – and a phenomenon that I actually had to see to believe. I'd been told about it when I started teaching and I was intrigued but sceptical. But when I was there, the absolute euphoria at the women-only Thursday night party, with groups of women singing and walking around the grounds, having had the most extraordinary consciousness-raising experience, was mesmerising. And if you didn't believe that more women would become lesbians given the opportunity, you would be hard pushed to deny it after seeing that.'

Scanlon saw the feminist teaching and the (mostly) women-only environment as a perfect combination for making lesbianism a positive choice, reinforcing Rich's view that there is a lesbian continuum, and that most women sit somewhere on that continuum if they allow themselves to experience the level of identification with other women which Rich calls the 'continuous but stifled theme which runs through heterosexual experience'. What she means is that women in relationships with men share common experiences, but rarely admit this to each other, or even to themselves. To acknowledge this is to understand the centrality of lesbianism to feminism in a visceral way, as Scanlon described to me: 'It didn't just come out of being in a women-only space; it came out of the conversations, it came out of the feminist politics, it came out of the fact that we were spending all day talking about women's experience, the joy and the pain of that. And then, as I say, no cooking, no kids, no cleaning, and then off to the bar, to thrash it all out, you know, into the early hours.'

The summer school was of its time – a time when women leaving heterosexual relationships for lesbian ones was rare enough to be remarkable. But the larger revelation was the way in which significant, life-changing decisions began to be made when women found themselves in situations where a different way of life looked possible – something they could not have conceived of before.

The 'experimental' lesbianism of today is commonplace. Same-sex attraction among women is acceptable, at least in cosmopolitan cities of the western world. Many celebrities have come out as lesbians. This change has come about largely because of the lesbian liberation movement, whose long, heroic campaigns shattered the stigma around lesbian relationships. Women are no longer likely to feel alarm or self-disgust at being drawn to someone of their own sex. Indeed, such a feeling is now often framed as exciting and intriguing. Women's stepping outside the narrow confines of heterosexual relationships is largely, at last, something to be celebrated.

## What Does 'Lesbian' Mean to Me?

### The diminishing hideousness of lesbians

When men (and women) repeat the derogatory stereotype that 'lesbians are ugly' it is both an anti-lesbian slur and a warning to heterosexual women. 'Look, those unfuckable, grotesque women must be lesbians,' say the misogynists; 'they are obviously trying to put men off.' It can be seen as a form of social control of all women, because we are socialised to please men, and to be liked. And this is nothing new.

Throughout the 20th century, lesbians had a dismal public image, epitomised by the predatory, unhinged, lonely, ugly and desperate character played by Beryl Reid in *The Killing of Sister George*. This stereotype has largely disappeared, even though many people, including some lesbians, remain reluctant to use the actual word 'lesbian'. Many of the 1990s lipstick lesbians called themselves 'gay'; lesbian feminists often prefer 'dyke', originally a term of abuse; and many young women now use the word 'queer' – a word with a terrible history, and which, of course, can be applied to men as well as women.

Stereotypes about lesbians being 'man-hating', 'damaged' and 'hyper-sexualised' (that's porn for you) are unpleasant and harmful, and over the years a number of women have told me that they hesitated to come out because of them. The unhinged, obsessive stalker or murderer is a lesbian trope across novels, films and television – a random selection: the lesbian characters in *Single White Female*, *Bound*, *Heavenly Creatures*, *Monster* and *Mulholland Drive*; Mrs Danvers in *Rebecca*, Barbara Covett in *Notes on a Scandal*. And, obviously, there are the *Lesbian Vampire Killers*. But today, feminism has turned the image of sad, mad, perverted and broken lesbians around, with characters such as Nan Astley in *Tipping the Velvet*, Yara Greyjoy in *Game of Thrones*, Poussey and Big Boo in *Orange is the New Black* and Anne Lister in *Gentleman Jack*. Lesbian-led narratives in mainstream film, television and novels now often show lesbianism as a positive choice for women.

## The lesbian renaissance

Thanks to feminism, the idea that a woman needs a man to provide for her economically has largely vanished, and with economic independence for women comes the freedom to explore different ways of having relationships and different ways of conducting their personal lives beyond (or instead of) traditional marriage.

When The Lesbian Project was launched in March 2023, Kathleen Stock, my co-director, wrote in the *Observer*, 'I had come out relatively late, at the end of my thirties. This was the defining moment of my life, changing everything in it for the better and sprinkling the world around me with Technicolor magic. I grabbed the label "lesbian" with both hands, viewing it as psychically connecting me with a world of exciting, bold, brave female adventurers and warriors before me, proudly doing their own special thing.'[6]

As we all know from our female friendships, women often have an instinctive understanding of each other. Many women discover that this brings emotional advantages to a lesbian relationship in comparison to a heterosexual one. It means that

## What Does 'Lesbian' Mean to Me?

lesbian relationships escape the kind of friction that arises in so many straight relationships: the rows over insensitivity, lack of engagement and failure to communicate. The same applies to sex, where women's understanding of female bodies can bring a heightened sense of physical sensitivity and mutual pleasure. Even Julie Burchill, a doggedly heterosexual journalist, once extolled the joys of 'girl-on-girl surfing' during an explosive affair with another female writer. It didn't last, sadly. (When I asked Burchill why she had not embarked on any other same-sex relationships, she said her foray into lesbianism had been like a visit to Iceland: great to do once, but not an experience she felt she needed to repeat.) And obviously there is no guarantee that a same-sex relationship will be less volatile or explosive than any other.

Most women who are involved in lesbian relationships feel very differently to Burchill. They find the intensity of the experience thrilling, and the level of mutual understanding profoundly moving. For too many women in heterosexual relationships, sex is still defined as thrusting penetration, despite Shere Hite's revolutionary and widely publicised research having revealed as long ago as the 1970s that this approach left many women unsatisfied and frustrated. And the problem with the male understanding of women's sexual pleasure has been made worse by the explosion of easily accessible pornography. Brutal, misogynistic imagery portrays women as dehumanised sex objects whose sole purpose is to fulfil men's desires with no apparent need for engagement or reciprocity. Combined with this is the dangerous misconception that women are turned on by such displays of often-violent machismo, a problem so widespread that rape counsellors in Scotland have warned that 'strangulation and "breath play"' have become so ubiquitous in online pornography that teenagers believe it is 'a routine sexual act they [are] expected to perform and enjoy'.[7] It is an uncomfortable fact that some women condone and even promote this kind of power play, harmful as it is. This does not make it any less misogynist, and nor does it mean that other women have to put up with it.

Thanks to feminist and lesbian campaigners, there is now a real alternative to this unbalanced world. A new realm of intimacy is available. As *Sex in the City* actor Cynthia Nixon once put it, 'I've been straight and I've been gay and I know which I prefer.'[8] And now, with the availability of donated sperm and the legal right to adoption, women no longer have to be in a relationship with a man in order to have children, so there is even more scope for women to be independent of men and live lesbian lives free of irresponsible, wayward, selfish or violent husbands and feckless, absent fathers for their children.

Visible lesbianism serves as a warning to heterosexual men. Lesbian liberation has given women a real and enticing alternative to heterosexuality. On Gay Pride marches of the past, I used to love it when the policemen stewards were heard muttering about the offensiveness of women who claimed they didn't need men. In response, we would taunt: 'Two, four, six, eight; is your missus really straight?'

## The inevitable backlash

Of course, with partial liberation comes a counteroffensive, and the latest form of attack on lesbians is the most insidious and dangerous yet. Trans activists, an umbrella term that takes in sexual libertarians, human rights organisations and so-called progressives, now want the definition of the word 'lesbian' expanded to include men.

'But you are against diversity,' trans activists claim, in order to argue for the inclusion of men in the category of lesbian. 'You might as well say you don't want black women in your groups either!' These accusations have been levelled at me and other women on a regular basis, and the analogy is clearly ridiculous and offensive, as many black women have pointed out. Whatever racism and exclusionary behaviour there may be within some lesbian groupings, black lesbians are not accused of not being women.

One example of this ludicrous line of argument has come from trans activist and academic Helen Clarke,[9] who claims that the LGB Alliance, set up in order to advocate for same-sex-attracted women and men in response to Stonewall redefining lesbians and gay men as 'same-gender-attracted', is 'a prime example of gender-critical feminism' because they believe that the '"sex-based" rights of those who are "same-sex-attracted" are threatened by the inclusion of trans individuals, and trans lesbians especially'. In other words, trans-identified men who claim to be lesbians are simply women with a difference, who face prejudice and exclusion by 'cis' lesbians. In one fell swoop, the fox becomes the chicken. Classic gaslighting.

The quote about the new 'lesbian bar' at the top of this chapter has the word 'lesbian' being used by all and sundry. But actual lesbians too are increasingly referring to themselves as queer, non-binary or even trans men. The fact is that every lesbian has one single thing in common: we are same-sex-attracted women, and we have the right to claim that label and that identity for ourselves. Those who are not lesbians do not have the right to ride roughshod over the meaning of the word nor tell us how to define ourselves. No man, ever, whether he is non-binary, trans identified or whatever, has the right to adopt this word to describe himself.

In June 2024, *Doctor Who* actor Matt Smith 'gently corrected' (according to the *Daily Mail*) the lesbian comedian and TV presenter Sue Perkins for using 'incorrect' pronouns for Emma D'Arcy, a female actor who identifies as non-binary and insists on the pronouns 'they/them' rather than the technically correct 'she/her'. For this, Smith received lavish praise from the virtue-signalling 'progressive' brigade (sample quote on social media: 'Matt correcting Sue on Emma's pronouns. OH MY HEART') – but what it comes down to is this: a heterosexual man implicitly chastised a lesbian for using the correct pronouns to describe a heterosexual woman. Perkins grovelled and apologised, posting on X/Twitter that she felt 'terrible' as she 'would never want to be disrespectful' to D'Arcy.

And one of the consequences of these linguistic acrobatics is that lesbians, *actual* lesbians, have been stripped of the right to claim that term as belonging to us and us alone, because if gender identity trumps biological sex, and anyone can identify as anything, it means 'non-binary' women who are attracted exclusively to other women reject the term 'lesbian' to describe themselves, because to be a lesbian means admitting to being a woman – unless you are a straight man who identifies as a woman, in which case he will co-opt it for himself. So, the term 'lesbian' has been bastardised by men and heterosexual women. While lesbians are being pressurised to use terms such as 'queer' or 'LGBTQ+' to describe ourselves, straight men have decided it will work as a new, cool word to describe the rainbow alliance. Unless we take it back, it will be lost to us forever. As Kathleen Stock explained, the aims of The Lesbian Project are 'to put lesbian needs and interests back into focus, to stop lesbians disappearing into the rainbow soup and to give them a non-partisan political voice. Same-sex-attracted females are not going anywhere, but public understanding of them is disappearing, and younger lesbians in particular are paying the price – however they identify, and whatever they call themselves. We think our task is urgent.'

In setting up the project, both Kathleen and I saw that any potential success would directly contribute to broader feminist efforts – and recognised that enhancing the rights and liberation of lesbians would have a positive impact on *all* women. Until women achieve the goal of full sexual autonomy – regardless of our sexual orientation – lesbians will remain oppressed and marginalised. Lesbianism and feminism are indivisible. We need each other.

# 2

# What's Feminism Got to Do with It?

## Why Lesbians Are Central to Women's Liberation

A lesbian is the rage of all women condensed to the point of explosion.

Radicalesbians

The true feminist deals out of a lesbian consciousness whether or not she ever sleeps with women.

Audre Lorde

I was having dinner with my partner Harriet and her favourite cousin, Joanne – an American whose 'alternative' lifestyle Harriet has always found appealing. As a young, bona fide bohemian in the 1960s, Joanne had been part of a famous hippy commune on Eel Pie Island in Twickenham. Even though she once described herself to me, with a wry smile, as 'irredeemably heterosexual', Joanne was critical of the conventional nuclear family structure and sought to subvert it – living communally, rejecting monogamy and helping to raise the children of Eel Pie.

The occasion was Joanne's 60th birthday, and she had invited some family and friends to dinner, including her best friend's daughter, a lesbian in her late twenties whom Joanne had known since birth, and her long-term partner; I will call them Sam and Jen. Over dinner, they talked about getting married if it became legally possible – this was 2009, four years before the Marriage (Same Sex Couples) Act came into force – and their desire to raise a family together.

Joanne entertained us with family memories of Harriet as a young lesbian, and Harriet chimed in with tales of our exploits when we first got together when we were about the same age as Sam and Jen. I described the very first direct action in which we had taken part, in 1988, in protest against Section 28, a series of UK laws which prohibited the 'promotion of homosexuality' by local authorities; we had stormed the London Ideal Home Exhibition and occupied a show home, unfurling banners with slogans such as 'Real, NOT pretend families' and 'Lesbians make great mothers'.

Joanne and most of her guests, who had lived through and joined in various adjacent political protests over the decades, were cheering along at the stories. But Sam and Jen seemed unmoved, and even a bit bored, as Harriet and I talked about how difficult it was to come out in the 1970s and described various early campaigns we had been involved in, including one which exposed how violent and abusive men who had been divorced by their wives were often granted custody of their children if their mothers had subsequently begun living as lesbians. I explained that, for me, fighting for lesbian liberation meant fighting for women's liberation. I told them about the battle to change the law so that same-sex couples could adopt and foster, and to make it illegal for employers to fire anyone for being lesbian or gay.

I was puzzled by Sam and Jen's apparent lack of interest in the conversation, but I thought maybe that as young people they didn't want to focus on the bad old days, even though our stories were about positive experiences of overcoming prejudice and bigotry. But then I realised that Sam was genuinely nonplussed by our tales. She explained her belief that progress was an inevitable force, and that the rights that she and Jen now enjoyed as lesbians had been an inevitable part of society's evolution. She said she really couldn't see the connection with activism, and seemed irritated that we assumed a degree of solidarity among lesbians past and present. For Jen, a police officer semi-out at work, being a lesbian was simply not an issue.

Of course, it is great that things have moved on since we were their age, but we were astounded that not only did this young couple have absolutely no grasp of or even interest in lesbian history, they also had no understanding of the notion that positive change for marginalised and oppressed groups happens only when individuals come together to demand it, rise up and say: 'We will not accept this any more.' Harriet asked whether they also assumed that apartheid in South Africa had ended 'organically', without campaigning and protest. Of course they didn't, they said. I could only assume that, for them, sexuality was a private matter concerning only the individual, whereas race was a matter of wider social justice.

I wasn't sure that we had changed their minds in the slightest. But a few years later, out of the blue, they got in touch with

Harriet. Now married and needing fertility treatment, they had encountered a problem because... they had been refused access to it as a same-sex couple. They wanted contact details for a feminist lawyer.

◆

Every single victory for lesbians, whether social, legal or political, happened because feminists, both lesbian and straight, recognised that lesbians were at the sharp end of society's misogyny, and because they saw that the theories developed by lesbian feminist writers such as Adrienne Rich and Kate Millett could apply to all women. Challenging the existing power structures would benefit everyone.

From Betty Friedan and her 'lavender menace' up until much more recently, there have been those within the feminist movement who have wanted lesbians to be invisible, in case their presence alienated 'ordinary women' or provoked the establishment and impeded the acceptance of the 'sensible agenda', such as free childcare, equal pay, and so on. Despite this, lesbians were the backbone of feminism's second wave, not least because they had more time to devote to the movement. In those days, unless they already had children from previous relationships with men, lesbians did not have families demanding their time and energy, and since many worked or volunteered around issues of violence against women they were profoundly aware of the urgency of the need for change. The various mainstream histories of the 1960s might not highlight this, but feminism and lesbianism were intimately interconnected in the political theory and activism of the Women's Liberation Movement. The freedoms enjoyed by lesbians today exist because of the battles that feminists fought and won across the US, Australia and New Zealand, and western Europe, in the 1960s, 1970s and 1980s.

## Along comes gender

In 2004, I wrote a column entitled 'Gender Benders, Beware' for the *Guardian Weekend* magazine, about what was happening to Vancouver Rape Relief (VRR) – Canada's longest-established women's shelter, and an impressive example of how lesbianism and feminism work in tandem. As a women's support and campaigning NGO, VRR had been targeted by transgender activists since the mid-1990s because it was unashamedly and uncompromisingly female-only. This small, grassroots, volunteer-led organisation was constantly under threat of losing its funding, and attacked on a regular basis for holding feminist views and refusing to compromise its founding principles.

I first heard of VRR in December 2003 when I saw a news report about a long-running legal battle the organisation had had with a trans woman named Kimberly Nixon. In 1995, Nixon, a former airline pilot who had lived as a man until the age of 33, applied to VRR to train as a counsellor for women who had experienced sexual violence. Nixon was rejected on the grounds that, since he had not experienced growing up female, he would not understand the impact of male violence and misogyny on the lives of the women who sought to access VRR services. With the support of the British Columbia Human Rights Tribunal, Nixon filed a formal human rights complaint, claiming that he had been discriminated against for being transgender. He won at the British Columbia Human Rights Tribunal, but VRR took the case to the Supreme Court of British Columbia, and in December 2003 the court decided there had been an error in judgment in the previous tribunal, and determined that VRR was not guilty of discrimination. This new judgment reasserted the group's right of freedom of association and reaffirmed that they had the right to decide on a women-only service.

In that *Guardian* article, I wrote: 'I don't have a problem with men disposing of their genitals, but it does not make them women, in the same way that shoving a bit of vacuum hose down your 501s does not make you a man.' The piece focused on my being a lesbian, and the constant pressure we are under, as lesbians, to conform to a stereotype. I bemoaned the fact that no sooner were lesbians getting somewhere in terms of being more confident in rejecting gender rules regarding how we 'should' dress and behave as women, than along comes a new, even more rigid, orthodoxy. 'Those who "transition" seem to become stereotypical in their appearance – fuck-me shoes and birds'-nest hair[1] for the boys; beards, muscles and tattoos for the girls,' I wrote. 'Think about a world inhabited just by transsexuals. It would look like the set of *Grease*.' (Yes, it was possible then not only to be frank and to the point – even slightly mocking, shock horror – about the ridiculous fiction of sex change, now called 'gender reassignment' or 'confirmation surgery', and for the *Guardian* to publish it.)

The emerging trans rights lobby encouraged members and allies to complain *en masse* to the Reader's Editor, Ian Mayes. Mayes' response, which appeared the following weekend, was almost as long as the original article. Headlined 'The Readers' Editor on... a column that did no favours for an often-abused minority', the piece, pandering to the trans lobby, was a knee-jerk reaction to the 200-plus complaints he had received. As far as Mayes was concerned, my article should probably not have been published. Conversely, Katharine Viner, then editor of the Saturday *Guardian* magazine supplement *Weekend*, gave the following comment: 'There are very many times that we disagree with our columnists, sometimes vociferously, but that is not the point – we are not looking for consensus... In this case, we thought that what Julie Bindel was writing was particularly interesting because it came from her – a lesbian activist for the rights of women and children... She is a rare kind of writer who puts her money where her mouth is.'

And there we have it: Viner – who had always been a feminist – totally understood my disquiet about the Kimberly Nixon attack on VRR.

Two years after my *Guardian* column was published, I was in a hotel lobby in Boston, Massachusetts, where I was having a drink with a few people with whom I had been to a feminist anti-pornography conference. I was telling the story of how the trans activists had begun to target me, when I felt a tap on my shoulder and heard the words, 'Are you Julie?' It was one of the rape relief collective from Vancouver, who happened to be at the same event. I was soon introduced to the rest of the delegation, and we became firm friends. Now, every opportunity I get, I visit Vancouver to see them, and I have been thrilled to speak at events hosted by VRR as well as the closely affiliated Vancouver Lesbian Collective (VLC).[2] When Justin Trudeau became prime minister in 2015, the gender madness and attack on lesbians and women in general in Canada became far more extreme because of this so-called progressive man's total capitulation to transgender ideology.

In 2015 I undertook a research project in Vancouver covering the city's missing and murdered women,[3] in particular those who disappeared from the city's Downtown Eastside, notorious for endemic pimping and drug abuse, along with disproportionate levels of homelessness, poverty and crime. Countless women, including underage girls, are caught up in the sex trade across Canada, but nowhere is the situation starker than here. The girls and women, many of whom come from indigenous communities, experience horrific violence and abuse, and services that can somehow connect to these women – terrified, hopeless, and usually addicted to crack cocaine and heroin – are precious. I was shown around one drop-in service by a small group of indigenous Canadian prostitution survivors who volunteer there and provide peer support among many other things, all funded on a shoestring.

But as I write, these services are barely functioning, and not only for want of money. Justin Trudeau, as well as regularly trotting out the 'trans women are women' mantra, also (inevitably) believes that 'sex work is work' and should be considered a job like any other. (The question of why, if this is so, women are unable to escape the clutches of the sex trade without exit services and very substantial support, of course goes unanswered.) Because of its ideological support for prostitution, a great deal of government time and energy is poured into normalising it – making it safer for johns and pimps, while claiming that this somehow benefits the terrorised women. This approach is based on no evidence – in fact, experts on sexual exploitation, including women who have escaped it, are clear that the women involved just want to get out.

Compounding the problem is the fact that gender ideology in Canada has been fully embedded in law. In Vancouver, men can declare themselves women and demand to be treated as such. It was in Vancouver in 2019 that Jessica 'wax my balls' Yaniv,[4] now known as Jessica Serenity Simpson, a trans woman, filed complaints against beauty salons run by women of immigrant background for having refused to provide him with a 'Brazilian' bikini wax (that is, the waxing of all hair from the female genital area). Given that this man (like the vast majority of trans women) retains his meat and two veg, the reason for their refusal is obvious. Yaniv lost – but only by the skin of his scrotum. The women lost too – in terms of both their livelihoods and their peace of mind. Lawyers representing a number of the women said they had suffered from depression, anxiety, insomnia and stress (which forced one of them to close her business) as a result of the court case and the accusations of bigotry and transphobia levelled at them by Yaniv and his representatives.

Vancouver's drop-in centres for prostituted women have been badly affected now that homeless men have realised they can use them by simply declaring themselves to be women. There is little staff can do about it. When I was shown around one particular centre, the first thing I saw was a group of bearded, boisterous men sitting around the communal table playing cards, loudly cursing each other. Slowly but surely, women have stopped using the centre, and the various other services set up by feminists have gone the same way.

When men are allowed into women's spaces, every female is affected. For lesbians, it means we are obliged to accept the presence – and tolerate the advances – of men who identify as women. During my most recent visit to Vancouver, in September 2023, I met with a number of lesbians who told me it is now impossible for them to hold autonomous public social gatherings unless they include 'trans lesbians'. The hold the men's rights movement has on Canada illustrates how the lives, rights and freedom of *all* women, lesbian and heterosexual alike, are curtailed by this backlash – and how counterproductive and politically incoherent it would be to separate out the issues. The situation in Canada is a cautionary tale about how we must avoid the separation of lesbians from other women. The misogynists certainly make little or no distinction between us when they attempt to justify their terrible actions and behaviour.

## Consciousness-raising: what is it good for?

One woman at the VLC told me, 'We've done some consciousness-raising groups where we talk about what we're proud of as lesbians, and try to promote that pride. And bearing in mind that we've had such bad press for so many years, actually saying to women in general that we have an awful lot to be proud of is liberating. It feels fantastic.'

Consciousness-raising gets a bad rap from those who misunderstand its purpose; for some, it is about identity politics and self-indulgence. In her review of Susanna Rustin's book, *Sexed: A History of British Feminism* (2024), Kathleen Stock bemoans the shift in focus away from 'the toughness, cleverness, and collaborative pragmatism of British women fighting on behalf of other women throughout the 18th, 19th, and early 20th centuries': 'By the time I arrived at [Rustin's] section on the Sixties and Seventies, things seemed to me to be going downhill... Suddenly everyone was consciousness-raising like mad – treating the new craze imported from the US as if groups of women had never discussed their circumstances and feelings together before – and becoming subtly beholden to a more volatile sensibility in the process. Despite the undoubted political and legal gains of this period, there was a growing shift of emphasis that looks ominous in retrospect: a move towards internal feelings and "subjectivity", and a fixation with how women were being culturally represented at the expense of other pressing concerns.'[5]

This representation of the 1960s and 1970s is a fundamentally inaccurate portrayal both of this period and of consciousness-raising as a feminist practice. It was developed as part of a feminist strategy in the early 1970s, when a wide recognition developed among feminists that women's voices were ranked below those of men. Women were patronised, silenced and ignored. Consciousness-raising allowed women to speak openly about intimate and difficult issues relating to violence and sexual abuse and enabled women to speak together about growing up as girls in a patriarchal society. At this stage, most women had not experienced these conversations with each other.

As the Women's Liberation Movement took off, many women on the political left were abandoning mainstream politics and instead getting into autonomous, women-only organising, campaigning about everything from abortion to equal pay, protesting male violence and setting up frontline services, along with holding consciousness-raising sessions, which served as a political tool, rather than a navel-gazing exercise. The personal was, truly, political.

By 1970, lesbian feminists were well and truly fed up with being in groups dominated by gay men and their interests, and felt that their natural home was within the Women's Liberation Movement. The words and actions of Betty Friedan at NOW were the final straw. The Lavender Menace Group, which later became the radicalesbians, one of whose number implied at the Columbia University event that Kate Millett was betraying the movement by not declaring herself a lesbian, promoted consciousness-raising among lesbians as a way of helping them to find the courage, support, solidarity and strength in numbers to speak out against compulsory heterosexuality. Without the sessions, these women would not have been able to speak openly – as their heterosexual sisters were beginning to – about their true feelings regarding men and sexuality. It was one thing for women to complain, as many did, about the lack of sexual satisfaction they experienced in relationships with men, but another altogether for women to say that they were sexually attracted to other women and *not men*.

Angela Wild is a lesbian feminist activist, artist, writer and founder member of the lesbian activist group Get The L Out, set up in the summer of 2018 to combat the rise of trans ideology within the so-called LGBTQ+ movement. For her, consciousness-raising was essential to escaping the heterosexual 'norm'. 'I started being involved in the gender war from a lesbian feminist perspective when I started calling myself a lesbian,' says Wild. 'It took me many years to be able to say that I wanted to be with women, that I loved women. There was no way that I was going to allow men to take away my right to define lesbianism as a woman who is attracted to other women, exclusively.'

Wild and other lesbians like her know that biology matters, and that no matter how connected to their 'feminine side' men claim to be, they are still men. Rather than fighting for the right to identify as women, they should be fighting for the freedom to express themselves as men, expanding the narrow confines of socially acceptable masculinity.

Lesbians are facing horrendous violence, bullying and discrimination as a result of gender ideology. We are being kicked off dating apps for stating a preference for biological women; having our physical spaces such as clubs and speed dating events invaded; and being banned from Pride events. But one of the major advantages to being a lesbian, certainly from my point of view, is that we do not have to navigate sexual relationships with men.

Those lesbians who demand that women acquiesce to the notion that 'trans women are women' – women such as comedian and writer Sandi Toksvig, publisher Linda Riley and former Stonewall CEOs Ruth Hunt and Nancy Kelley – are betraying heterosexual women as well as lesbians. These lesbians march under the banner of 'L with the T' and call themselves 'trans inclusive'. They refer to lesbians that refuse to accept that some men can be lesbians as 'transphobic', and publicly denounce us.

Transgender ideology acts as a smokescreen for those men with particular kinks that women are then expected to put up with. For example, before the institutionalised acceptance of transgenderism in men, stealing a woman's underwear in order to masturbate into it would've been seen as a deeply unpleasant crime. But in today's queer world, this type of behaviour and 'kink' is not only normalised but celebrated.

Heterosexual women who suddenly find themselves living with trans-identified men are not even granted the status of 'victim', despite having to cope with sexual violation, bullying and gaslighting. These women have spoken out about the horrors of being coerced into accepting the actions of autogynephilic men, as trans activists promote the falsehood that they are bigots and 'transphobes' if they refuse to accept these men as women. As Grace,[6] a woman whose long-term male partner declared himself out of the blue to be a woman, describes to me: 'He told me we were now a lesbian couple. I thought to myself, "If I wanted to be a lesbian I would choose an actual woman – someone with a female body, without a scratchy five o'clock shadow, and who smells like a woman and not some sweaty man. To pretend he is female would repulse me."'

Do lesbians, who have been told we are transphobic and 'genital fetishists' for refusing to consider trans-identified males as sexual partners, really think it is OK to tell women like Grace that she should cave in to pressure and redefine her sexual orientation?

Lesbians who declare themselves to be part of the LGBTQ+ rainbow, and claim to be 'trans inclusive', rarely, it would appear, have sexual relationships with men claiming to be women. Why, then, should their straight counterparts?

## Feminist views on gender

Back in the heady days of second-wave feminism, the concept of gender was central to feminist thinking. Defined as distinct from biology, it was viewed as a social construct that equates masculine with male and feminine with female. Feminists understood the concept as leading directly to oppression, an obstacle to women's equality that we wanted to abolish. As second-wave feminists, we were trying to construct our political theory around our activism, and make the development of theory both relevant and accountable to the movement. It was a fundamental tenet of our politics that all things concerning gender were socially constructed – starting with the suffocating rules imposed on both male and female behaviour. But I now wonder if, in our focus on the social construction of gender, we lost sight of sexual difference altogether. So anxious were we to minimise the significance of any biological differences between men and women that we almost ended up ignoring the fact that we inhabited bodies at all. While we were busy arguing that women could do pretty much everything that men could, we (recklessly, or so it seems now) threw the biological baby out with the gender bathwater, inadvertently opening up a gap through which postmodernism and the likes of Judith Butler were able to get in. The postmodernists (forerunners of today's 'queer theorists') might have dismissed biology, but in a way that was significantly different from the feminist position. In her 1990 book *Gender Trouble*, which arguably did more damage to the feminist cause than any book published in the last 50 years, Butler conflated sex and gender into 'performance'. She writes, 'When the constructed status of gender is theorized as radically independent of sex, gender itself becomes a free-floating artifice.' For Butler, the category of 'woman' is 'fluid'. This means that women have nothing in common, and anyone can join the club.

Feminists, on the other hand, deconstructed gender as a set of social rules (rather than the more benign 'roles') which females are required to obey or face punishment. Feminists address the material reality of women's oppression and have little patience with notions of 'performativity' when it comes to masculinity and femininity. They prefer the classic definition of women that makes sense to most people, and believe lesbians are being discriminated against, at best, by the rise of 'queer'. And the gender movement presents, as ever, a confused argument: on the one hand, 'people are who they say they are', and it is perfectly possible for a woman and indeed a lesbian to look very much like a man with a beard and a penis; on the other, 'transition' can require lifelong medication and radical surgery for those who 'need' it. So we feminists now find ourselves having to argue, repeatedly, that the biological differences between men and women are significant. Feminists had long considered one of our major achievements to have been establishing the difference between biological sex and gender. Now that gender is celebrated as a key feature of individual identity and actively propagated and promoted as though it is in itself a legally protected characteristic (clue: it's not), it would be fair to say that we were premature in our belief that we had won the argument. The genderists and the reactionaries are both keen, for their own reasons, to police women's behaviour. Feminists both lesbian and straight need to be vocal about this sinister and dangerous agenda.

### What's Feminism Got to Do with It?

I interviewed my old friend Lynn Alderson, a lesbian activist and a founder, in 1978, of the legendary Sisterwrite bookshop, café and feminist event space in Islington. Alderson observed accurately that 'Young lesbians have no exposure to feminism, which is how it has become a dirty word among many of them.' She went on to say that 'Every generation of women seems to be cut off from the next.' She is right. Whatever feminists achieve, it seems inevitable that the next generation of women grows up disliking what their predecessors stood for, because they are so overwhelmingly characterised as sexless, humourless, unattractive prudes, and/or hairy, aggressive monsters. 'These are the portrayals of feminists in the media, and for a lot of young women, that's scary', says Alderson. 'They don't want to identify with older women either – none of us did when we were young. But it means that there's this severing, so that each generation has to rebuild these things all over again. And the loss of that feminist continuity costs women greatly, and I think it's cost this generation of women greatly.'

## The importance of feminism in lesbian culture

As I began researching this book I was delighted to be contacted out of the blue by Ingrid Nyeboe, who, as I mention in the introduction, is the widow of Jill Johnston. 'I meant to thank you at the time for Jill's obituary,' she wrote. Jill had died in 2010, and I was delighted when my pitch to write about her life was accepted by the *Guardian*. Ingrid and I arranged to speak, as I was fascinated to hear about Jill's life from a fellow lesbian and feminist who had known her for many decades.

At the time the women got to know each other, Johnston had a column in the *Village Voice*, an influential publication which was widely read. 'Once Jill and I got together, which happened during 1978–79, she would be stopped on the street and somebody would just run into her and say, "Oh, I have to thank you. You saved my life. I went to that. I saw that. I've heard you. And it changed how I felt about myself."'

I ask Nyeboe her views on the lesbian politics of today, and she tells me that as far as she is concerned, there is 'no radicalism left in the majority of lesbians because they think that they have gotten to where they're supposed to get to, and that's as far from the truth as you can get'. During our Zoom call, during which Nyeboe recalls fascinating details about the lesbian community and politics of 1970s New York, she muses as to how things are now:

'I think it happens with all political revolutionary movements, the larger society expands and swallows as much of you as possible,' she says, 'and spits you out in *The L Word* [a glossy US television series about lesbians and bisexuals in Los Angeles], or whatever else they put together that looks OK, but not dangerous.'

Just as its treatment of lesbians can be an index of the levels of sexism and misogyny in any given society, the strength and vibrancy of feminist politics in any society will be reflected in the presence of a thriving lesbian culture.

'We are great, and we are good for each other,' says Jo from the Sitka Lesbian Housing Cooperative in Vancouver – an amazing resource I visited in September 2023. 'I like the fact that we retain close friendships with women that we've been in relationships with, that we've been married to, that we have sexually desired but it hasn't gone anywhere, and yet still have each other in our lives. We morph into those friendships, or we begin as friends and sometimes it becomes more of a sexual or romantic relationship. It's unique and it's precious and beautiful.'

Feminism is the foundation of lesbian culture. Without a feminist analysis, how would we understand lesbianism, as same-sex-attracted females? Our sexuality would be something we had no choice in or power over – and thus, not a source of pride. We would be left either searching for answers as to why we are different from the 'norm', bemoaning fate for making us the way we are, trying desperately to change, or begging to be assimilated into conventional straight society. For Alderson, 'The key thing for me, really, is my definition of myself as a feminist. I think that's the guiding light... I could never disentangle my life from that.' For her, the difference between a lesbian existence with no understanding of who we are or why we are hated, and the sort of lesbian life she went on to live, was feminism. 'Lesbian feminism, for me, was all about understanding your place in the world as a woman, understanding what oppression did to you both as a woman and as a lesbian.'

I agree. The accusation of lesbianism – and it *is* an accusation, make no mistake – is a way of influencing, and even controlling, the behaviour of all women. Many heterosexual women who reject a feminist analysis of this type of behaviour adhere to feminine beauty standards in part because they don't want to be accused of being lesbian. These women would likely not even consider working in manual trades in case they are accused of being lesbian. They avoid going regularly to women-only spaces for fear that men will assume they are lesbian.

## *Lesbians*

As Sandra McNeill, veteran feminist, proud lesbian, and campaigner against male violence towards women said to me back in my teenage years, when I was struggling to appreciate how and why women like her celebrated being lesbian, 'Being a lesbian is a privilege, not an oppression.' She was not dismissing the prejudice, bigotry and violence that so many of us are familiar with: as a woman born in Scotland in 1949, she has experienced her fair share. What she meant was that being a lesbian is great *in itself*. Jo again: 'We value our connections, and we tend to be able to work through shit. So if it didn't work as partners, OK, but I still love you and I want you in my life, and so we get to be best friends. I have one ex who lives across the hall from her two exes who got together.'

Lesbian culture, friendship networks and relationships are – for the most part – so rewarding, affirming and exhilarating that it's no wonder some men feel threatened by them and seek to destroy them. Neither is it any wonder that the most common form of social control of lesbianism is silence and invisibility – if the truth got out, it might spread! Instead, women who seek the approval of men volunteer to do the work of patriarchy themselves: it is a sad truth that many women on the left, and even some of those engaged in feminist politics, were unwilling to support lesbians when we first articulated concerns about the trans rights movement. Why was this? Maybe because they chose not to see how it affected lesbians directly, and failed to see how it affected all women.

I speak to Angela Wild, who I have known from the UK feminist movement for some years, during which time she noticed that many lesbians were alive to the threat of gender ideology. Some, she says, ignored the threat until significant damage had been done, whereas others were alert to it early on. 'There were several instances where we were portrayed as the bad guys because we raised it,' says Wild. 'And I don't want to really go after these women, because eventually they saw it, but it felt really bad at the time; it felt like a betrayal.'

## Critics of gender ideology

Here is a claim published in a paper in May 2023 in the *Journal of Lesbian Studies* about the 'anti-gender' movement: 'While some strands of gender-critical politics are openly allied with far-right politics and are explicitly anti-feminist, others include prominent figures from left-wing positions, including left feminists and lesbians. Challenging gender-critical politics in Britain requires a reckoning with its cross-political nature and an analysis of the factors that unite these different strands across left and right.'[7] The abstract of the article also contains the doubtless good-faith question, 'Does Britain's gender critical feminism directly align with the global trends of anti-gender mobilisations, including the latter's authoritarian and neofascist tendencies?'

This is extraordinary. It is true that what might loosely be described as 'gender-critical' (or 'sex-realist') feminists exist across the mainstream political spectrum. But the suggestion that 'far-right' opponents of transgenderism can be described as 'gender-critical' – and that there is something that 'unites' these diametrically opposed positions – is rubbish. The reality is that people from left and right can share the same perspective on some issues while completely disagreeing on others, just as traditional conservatives sometimes embrace the idea of the trans child rather than face life with a camp son or tomboy girl who might be gay. This situation reminds me of the days when feminists campaigning against the exploitation of women in the sex trade were told we were working 'hand in hand' with the religious right, who objected to obscenity and nudity and were pro-censorship. Most right-wingers are great believers in enforcement of the strictly 'gendered' behaviours that feminists refer to as sex stereotypes, and their disapproval of gender non-conformity is wholesale. In other words, right/far-right critics of what feminists refer to as 'gender ideology' object to it because it enables men and women to reject prescribed ways of dressing and behaving. These are people who are very attached to the notions of what a 'real man' and a 'real woman' look like, and would tend to view a butch-presenting lesbian as something other than a 'real woman' – and thus, unacceptable.

Some of the anti-feminist men and women who focus exclusively on the gender issue like to mock both lesbians and gay men for not conforming to sex stereotypes, such as when Billy Porter wore a full-length velvet skirt at the Oscars, explaining to *Vogue*, 'This look was interesting because it's not drag. I'm not a drag queen, I'm a man in a dress.'[8] Such people seem to be personally insulted by men in feminised apparel – high heels, make-up, elaborately styled hair, and bright colours – deriding them for embracing the accoutrements of femininity that they associate with womanhood. I too feel insulted by men who dress up as parodies of women – but to me it isn't personal. I'm insulted as a feminist – as someone who, along with women from many nations and cultures, has fought long and hard not to be pressurised into wearing such clothes, or constructing our appearance in this way. But to me, the likes of Billy Porter magisterially subvert gender norms, unlike drag queens, who are mocking women and using the sexist stereotypes feminists are in the business of abolishing for fun. When I hear trans activists accuse feminists objecting to trans women wearing parodically 'feminine' outfits of being 'essentialist' it profoundly irritates me. 'What about David Bowie/Grace Jones/Boy George/Suzi Quatro?' they ask, as though because all of the above were known as 'gender benders' to a greater or lesser degree, the question is a kind of 'gotcha'. But none of these individuals has ever, to my knowledge, described themselves as being of the opposite sex to their own – indeed that was the point of their presentation, as it was the point of Billy Porter's beautiful gown. Subverting gender rules (or sex stereotypes as feminists tend to call them) is positive. Mocking the insignia of women's oppression, such as men wearing inflated fake breasts, hooker outfits and garish make-up, is a whole other matter.

The role of feminism in the rise to prominence of gender ideology is much disputed. Reactionaries often blame those they vaguely refer to as 'feminists', without distinguishing between the 'queer intersectional feminists' in academia and actual grassroots feminist lesbian activists. So-called academics and intellectuals such as Sally Hines, Alison Phipps and Judith Butler claim to be feminists (and in Butler's case, also a non-binary lesbian – no, me neither), but are keen to dissociate themselves from feminists, lesbian and straight, who reject gender ideology. I am not the arbiter of who is and isn't a feminist, and definitions are up for debate of course, but words do have to mean *something*.

Let's take Hines first. In December 2018 she tweeted, 'Very much looking forward to a lovely lazy Xmas break and then to cracking on with my article about why "sex" (as in "biological" not desire) is no longer applicable to contemporary feminist theory inductivism.' The following March, Hines claimed, again in the form of a tweet, that 'Before the Enlightenment, the female skeleton didn't exist', which forms part of her argument that biological sex is totally irrelevant in all contexts, and gender identity is the only characteristic that matters. Hines had previously posted, 'Social, cultural and economic conditions and ideologies create oppression, exploitation, sexism not biology. It's the politics we place on perceived biological materialities that bring about patriarchy not bodies themselves.' In response to some pushback, Hines went on to say that 'No one without an anti-trans agenda says female anymore. People say woman.' Are these the words of a feminist as anyone understands the term?

Alison Phipps is the author of a book entitled *Me, Not You: The Trouble with Mainstream Feminism* (2021),[9] and she could easily have replaced the word 'mainstream' with the word 'white'. Her argument seems to be that anyone who is both black and a woman (by which she means anyone who identifies as a woman, including men) is always right about everything. She also makes clear that feminists who won't refer to violent sexual exploitation of women by men as 'sex work', or don't buy the 'trans women *are* women' line, are 'bad women' – and, by default, racist white feminists, regardless of their actual ethnicity. Phipps – who is white – predictably recuses herself from this 'white feminist' category, because the label has no connection with your lived experience as a black or white woman – in much the same way as being a woman is a label that has no relationship to your lived experience, but is rather an identity you can put on or take off. She writes: 'Privileged white women use their traumatic experiences to create media outrage and rely on state power and bureaucracy to purge "bad men" from elite institutions with little concern for where they might appear next.'

This is a woman who calls herself a feminist talking about women who have reported men to the police for the crimes of rape and other forms of violence against women. Phipps seems to be suggesting that it is somehow wrong to use the criminal justice system to tackle sexual predators, and that when 'privileged white' women 'purge' dangerous men from their workplaces and communities they *do not care* if these men decide to rape impoverished black women instead. For those of us who campaign for the criminalisation of those men who are a danger to women, the whole point of supporting 'carceral measures' is that putting men in prison means they are not free to go and commit crimes against a different section of the population, a point that seems to escape Phipps.

And finally, to Judith Butler. During a public event in San Francisco in June 2024, the lesbian feminist campaigner Amanda Kovattana asked Judith Butler a question about trans women accessing female-only spaces. This is Kovattana's account, posted on her Substack: 'I asked, "If gender is to liberate us, why can't I, as a lesbian, have a dick-free space? A space that is for women only, without penises?" [Butler] answered, "You can have such a space at home, unless you have a son." Then she proceeded to school me on my presumed fears, that as a feminist I must think more about where violence comes from. That the penis is not the source of violence. And I should not reduce people to anatomical parts. The audience applauded her. That's when it was clear to me she was leading a men's rights movement. Men fawn all over her for this.'[10]

Where to begin? No feminist, lesbian or otherwise, has to my knowledge claimed that the penis is dangerous in and of itself. Yet it is undeniably true that a penis attached to a violent, abusive man is routinely used as a weapon; it is impossible to ignore its significance in that context.

The beliefs advocated by Hines, Phipps and Butler are among those that have given rise to the accusations that lesbians are transphobic bigots, biological essentialists, or even 'sexual racists' if we deny that trans women are women and assert our right not to have a sexual relationship with a man with (or indeed without) a penis who says he is a woman. And this hardcore trans ideology is not just bonkers; as we will see, it can and does put women in real danger.

In March 2019, Angela Wild published a report entitled 'Lesbians at Ground Zero',[11] based on interviews with 80 lesbians[12] about their experiences of the so-called 'cotton ceiling' – a term coined by men identifying as 'trans lesbians' in reference to their difficulties being accepted as sexual partners by lesbians. The statistics in the report make for sobering reading. Two-thirds of respondents reported having been intimidated or having received threats from within their LGBTQ+ groups for rejecting the idea that men can be women, and some women had been raped by trans women. When the findings were reported in a BBC Online article in 2021, such was the vitriol from trans activists that more than 16,000 people signed an open letter calling for an apology from the corporation.

'There is this element of erasing the meaning of words,' Wild tells me. 'It's not just the trans activists who believe themselves to be on the left who do it. The right do it too, when they declare that any structural analysis based on race or sex is "woke", and therefore to be dismissed. And that is a right-wing *and* an anti-feminist agenda.'

Many of us had been consoling ourselves with the idea that the mainstream attitude towards lesbians had started to change for the better. But now the far right are saying the same blatantly sexist and misogynistic things they have always said, except now we are told that some 'women's rights activists' agree with them. 'It's very twisted. The anti-woke movement is basically a rejection of any structural analysis,' says Wild. 'And so they also reject feminism, calling it woke.' The political landscape in which we are now operating as feminists is more complicated than it has ever been, and the transgender lobby exploits that complexity, using it to foment the confusion and division which is advantageous to their cause. Wild is also critical of the way the conflict between women's rights and trans rights is positioned as one of left versus right, even though second-wave feminists realised long ago misogyny isn't exclusive to either. She believes that only feminists truly see that no one can help us but ourselves.

The right embrace men like Matt Walsh, who believe we have brought this madness on ourselves. As he put it in his 2022 film,

*What Is a Woman?*, 'You wanted men to be just like women, or women to be equal to men.' This argument has something in common with my own uneasiness about the erasure of sexual difference, which is, ironically, what makes it so insidious. But Walsh is wrong. As Wild observes, this is 'a completely twisted way to look at it, and it is untrue. Feminists have always opposed sexist stereotypes, which we call gender. I'm afraid that the backlash which is coming [from the political right and from non-feminist women activists] is very visibly an anti-gay and lesbian backlash. This lot, they will put everybody in the same bag, and then we're just going back to very traditional values.'

Nicole Jones is an artist, lesbian and feminist living in Edinburgh. She has found, in progressive, upper- and middle-class contexts, that some lesbians are quite hostile to feminism. She believes this is because lesbian feminism is thought to signify 'transphobia'. She told me, 'I think that a lot of my experience of the lesbian scene is actually just gay male, and a lot of the language (like bottom/top) is the power dynamics; lesbians seem to have adopted these terms. I remember once I was talking to somebody who, when she found out I was a lesbian, said, "Oh have you seen RuPaul?" – this was the first thing she said! And then I said no. And she says, "Oh, so you're gay, but you're not *that* gay." And when I said, "No, more like dyke," she said, "Oh, I feel masculine too sometimes."' This exchange is very revealing about the state of 'gay politics' and culture versus lesbian feminism.

If feminist analysis was suddenly entirely absent from issues relating to lesbian identity, culture and politics, we would be just another sexual minority, rather than the only group of women around the globe, within every culture and community, that is *not* defined in relation to men. If we reject feminism, we reject the very basis on which we fight for our true liberation. If we think that because we are now to some extent tolerated in western society and have achieved equal legal rights we are now liberated, then we are massively short-changing ourselves; true liberation for lesbians would offer us so much more.

Bernadette McDonald is 73 years old and has been involved in lesbian feminist politics for several decades. We meet at a conference in Montreal, Canada, where the topic is the sex trade. We chat between sessions at a small table in a quiet corner. 'I am so grateful that we did not grow up with this ideology over our heads,' says McDonald, tapping the table for emphasis. 'Right now, for the first time, I feel threatened as a lesbian. I ask myself, "Is it safe to come out to these people as criticising trans ideology?" Progressives can't be seen to hate me because I'm a lesbian. But they're not going to see me as progressive any more. And so I've been very careful who I talk to, because I don't want to be cancelled.'

I suggest to her that while trans ideology certainly is waging war against the very material basis of lesbian rights, it is also incredibly damaging to feminist activism in general.

McDonald agrees. 'The deep misogyny in this ideology is beyond anything I have ever imagined,' she says. 'How did I not see this coming? How hard did I try to stop the young lesbians I have mentored from taking the trans route? I mean, some of them are now taking hormones and having surgery. I want them to come and celebrate being lesbians, and not feel like they have to change their bodies and pretend to be men. It is the opposite of pride, and flies in the face of a feminist understanding of women's oppression.'

## Lesbian liberation – what has gone wrong?

The first letter of the LGBTQ+ banner might be the L, but it has turned out to stand for 'last in the queue'.

When it *should* have been our turn for a little attention (for what it would have been worth) from the likes of Stonewall, the 'lesbians with penises' were prioritised. We should be in the midst of a revolution that challenges gender norms and dismantles patriarchy. Instead, we are living in a world where commercial assisted reproduction is being touted as a human rights issue for lesbians, and from what I hear from many young lesbians I have spoken to as part of various projects over the past five years, there is even more anti-lesbian bullying in schools and punishment rape of young lesbians than there was when I came out more than 40 years ago.

The fights against gender ideology and against the sexist stereotyping of women are one and the same, and clarify how anti-lesbianism and sexism are two sides of the same coin. We need a revolution for lesbians and for all women right now, and it starts here.

# 3

# Why and How We Are Hated

> If you want to measure how much misogyny there is in any one society, look at how lesbians are viewed and treated. All women experience sexism, but for lesbians, it is supercharged – sexism on stilts.
>
> Annie, lesbian activist, Australia, 2023

> When a trans woman who has experienced transphobic behaviour from lesbians says, 'Lesbians are transphobic,' she is not redefining the lesbian identity as transphobic, but expressing her lived experience of oppression in an acceptably challenging way... No lesbian should take that as a personal attack or an attack on the lesbian identity. Someone who does is experiencing cis fragility and is effectively saying #NotAllLesbians.
>
> Chris Babcock, self-described disabled trans and queer activist, writing on Medium, October 2015[1]

In 1980, when I was living in the YWCA hostel in Leeds with Diane, we had no money. Trainee hairdressers, even at high-end salons, didn't earn much. And she had had to take time off sick, having been pushed close to a breakdown by the behaviour of some of her colleagues. Diane was both the only black person and the only out lesbian at the salon. While gay men were celebrated in the hairdressing world, black lesbians were most certainly not.

## Lesbians

One evening, we were caught shoplifting food in the local supermarket. We had nicked enough for our dinner that night, and thought we had got away with it but were nobbled outside by a security guard. The police came, we were held at the station for hours, and then bailed to appear in court a few days later.

Prior to our names being called to go in front of the magistrate, a probation officer – he was a youngish, smartly dressed man – came to see us in the waiting room. I remember what happened next like it was yesterday. He took out an envelope in which there was a strip of photographs of me and Diane from a photo booth, in which we were kissing. The probation officer looked pointedly at the pictures, then at each of us and said, 'Is there anything you want to tell me?' I knew he was asking me to confirm that Diane and I were in a relationship, but I couldn't for the life of me figure out how this was relevant to a shoplifting charge. Then he said, 'It's obvious that things are very wrong at home. I can put forward an argument for leniency, if only you would tell me what it is that has led you to this way of life?'

We asked for the photographs back, and went to face the court. The magistrate issued a fine for the theft of a tin of peas, two lamb chops, and a packet of cheese slices. On the way out, the probation officer opened the door from the courtroom and said, 'I do hope the pair of you get the help you so obviously need.' He definitely did not mean a rehabilitation programme to address our shoplifting.

Although Diane and I often laughed about the probation officer, wondering if he put as much time and effort into reforming petty criminals who didn't appear to be sexual deviants, it left a dusty taste in my mouth. This man had tried to persuade us both to tell him that we were mentally unwell and couldn't help ourselves – the evidence being that our relationship was to him some kind of perverted dalliance. I did wonder what would have happened had we been committing a more serious crime. In fact, when I was arrested a few months later for criminal damage at a porn cinema – I was part of a feminist protest, and all we did was throw a few eggs at the screen before being escorted out – there was no mention by security, or by the police during the time I was in custody, of the fact that the group of us carrying out this direct action were all very clearly lesbians, covered in badges declaring ourselves to be 'Dykes' and the inhabitants of a 'Lesbian Nation'.

What must have thrown the probation officer was the fact that two young women – looking no different from any other – would make do with each other, when there were plenty of eligible men out there.

◆

## Some things have changed...

Since coming out as a lesbian at the age of 15 in 1977, I have seen the world change for the better. But over the decades since then, I have also seen and experienced anti-lesbian violence first-hand. I have been attacked on more than one occasion – physically assaulted by anti-gay bigots, and sexually assaulted by a man who thought he could 'straighten me out'. I've lost both housing and work because I am a lesbian.

The first time I was physically attacked was at Rockshots in Newcastle, a gay and lesbian bar. I was 16, and out with

David – a gay friend who had taken me under his wing. We were dancing and laughing, having great fun. David was encouraging me to talk to other girls, but I was too shy. Suddenly, a small group of men was upon us, pointing their fingers in our faces. One of them asked David, 'Are you a poof?' Another growled, 'Prove you're a proper man and fuck her,' pulling me over to David by my hair. I was terrified, and David started crying. Other people saw what was happening – but no one came to our aid. The men were menacing, with shaven heads and dressed in combat gear. I lived close to a garrison town, and sexual assaults by soldiers in the vicinity were commonplace. After a few minutes of being hauled around by my arms and my hair, while David was jabbed in his stomach and groin, the men spat at us and left the club, laughing. David and I never spoke of the incident – I suspect he felt the same deep shame and stigma I did.

Leeds, where I lived next, was far more diverse than my home town, but had become a key base for a group of fascists known as Combat 18 (the numbers 1 and 8 representing the numerical order of Adolf Hitler's initials in the alphabet). The windows of the YWCA where Diane and I lived were regularly broken by young fascist males, and graffiti was daubed on our front door. One evening, we were chased through a park by skinheads brandishing chains, shouting that they were going to 'skin and rape' the 'black bastard' and her 'n*****-loving queer'. We escaped into a neighbour's house, where we had to endure a lecture on how we had brought 'trouble to the neighbourhood'. This neighbour also demanded to know if we really had to 'shove it [what we were] down everyone's throats'?

## Why and How We Are Hated

At the time, I had a job cleaning in a gay and lesbian bar run by a straight couple, Stan and Annie, and their son, Robert. Having retired from the police, Stan and Annie had spotted a financial opportunity in catering to the many lesbians and gay men who had gravitated to the city from the surrounding rural areas and small towns. 'The queers have loads of money,' Stan used to say. 'They don't have kids to feed.' One day, when I was cleaning the apartment above the pub, Stan and Robert attempted to rape me. They were laughing, telling me I needed a 'good fuck'. I managed to escape only because they heard Annie coming up the stairs.

I have been attacked or endangered by men who targeted me for being a lesbian numerous times. I have been thrown down the stairs by a nightclub bouncer. I have been punched in the face by a man in the street for refusing his advances. I learned to fight back and stay out of nightclubs – and to view these attacks as part of a misogynistic backlash by men who felt threatened by women's sexual and social autonomy.

Surely, after decades of lesbian and feminist campaigning, things are significantly better for young lesbians coming out today, and for all we lesbians who live our lives openly, without shame? In many ways that is true, but it's also true that we face new and even more insidious challenges to our hard-won rights and liberties.

### How anti-lesbian hatred reinvented itself

Forty-one years after I moved to Leeds, during a 2023 trip to Toronto to research this book, I met Olga,[2] a woman in her early twenties who had moved from Ukraine to Canada. Olga is a lesbian whose family back home initially wanted her to undergo conversion therapy to turn her straight and then, when she was 17, took her to an endocrinologist because her father had heard that taking oestrogen could make women become attracted to men. 'He pretty much told the doctor to make me normal,' she told me. 'It would stop me being what he called "anti-social". I was insomniac and had PTSD following an abusive relationship. I told [the clinician] that I wanted to die, that's all I wanted to do. And they're like, "Are you sure you don't want to be a man? You look pretty masculine."'

The clinicians were aware that Olga was same-sex-attracted, and they told her, 'If you prefer women, and you're a woman yourself, you should transition and become a man.' Within two weeks, she had begun the process. Olga had six appointments ('at the most') with a psychiatrist, during which she was asked questions about things like which toys she had liked playing with as a child. 'I said, of course, cars,' Olga recalls, 'and they said, "So you're a boy! Go for it!"'

Olga was given a prescription for testosterone and referred to a surgeon to discuss her options. Thankfully, she didn't go ahead with it. After three and a half years on testosterone, Olga admitted to herself that it had all been a terrible mistake: 'I stopped taking testosterone. I called my psychiatrist and asked if the name and sex on my documents could be changed back. And they told me, sorry, we don't have such a procedure in Ukraine at all. So, bye.

'I was born and raised in the eastern part of Ukraine,' says Olga, stirring her hot chocolate vigorously, 'in an extremely conservative small town. And I was constantly bullied for being a lesbian. And I thought, well, maybe it's better to be a man in order to not be bullied. But being able to reject that trans identity that I was conditioned into, and get back to my lesbian one, is the best, most liberating thing that's ever happened to me.'

## There's nothing new about anti-lesbian propaganda

Anti-lesbian bigotry has long been challenged by feminists and lesbian liberationists, and huge strides have been made in the campaign for lesbian rights, but in recent years, anti-lesbian stereotypes have returned with a vengeance. In large part, we have Stonewall and similar organisations to thank for this development. Butch-presenting lesbians, or women who merely reject stereotypically 'feminine' clothing and presentation, as well as many young women still trying to figure out who they are, have been railroaded into adopting transgender identities and groomed into believing they are trapped in the wrong body. This is the very antithesis of lesbian liberation; it can accurately be described as lesbian elimination.

When it is not being appropriated, our identity is being dismissed entirely, and not just by the tedious straight men who 'joke' that, as they are sexually attracted to women, they must be lesbians themselves. In 1921, a Criminal Law Amendment Bill came before Parliament which among other things strengthened age of consent laws; an amendment was tabled which added a new offence of gross indecency between women. Had it been passed by Parliament, then all sexual activity between women would have been illegal. The original Criminal Law Amendment

Act of 1885 had contained similar provisions criminalising sexual activity between women as well as between men. The story goes that Queen Victoria withheld royal assent until this provision was removed, arguing that 'women do not do such things'. But even the queen-empress did not have the power to block legislation passed by Parliament. The exclusion of lesbians from the Act was in fact a deliberate act of erasure by the all-male legislature. And during the 1921 debate on the same matter, a Conservative MP named Lieutenant Colonel Moore-Brabazon had the following suggestions to make as to how lesbianism should be 'dealt with':

'The first is the death sentence. That has been tried in old times, and, though drastic, it does what is required. That is, stamp them out. The second is to look upon them frankly as lunatics, and lock them up for the rest of their lives. That is a very satisfactory way also. It gets rid of them. The third way is to leave them entirely alone, not notice them, not advertise them. That is the method that has been adopted in England for many hundred years.'

In the event, the Bill ran out of time.[3] Lesbians remained officially non-existent. Of course, Moore-Brabazon and his cronies knew perfectly well that lesbianism was a thing – which is precisely why they decided not to accord it the official status it would have gained via criminalisation. But the mythology that grew out of these events persists. People still airily explain to me that lesbians have never suffered systematic discrimination and abuse at the hands of the state because Queen Victoria refused to believe in our existence.

There were of course indirect ways of prosecuting lesbians. In the mid-18th century, a handful of upper-class female couples masqueraded as husband and wife in order to be able to live safely as a couple, and found themselves in court (about half a dozen 'female husband' prosecutions were reported in the press), but the charges tended to relate to fraud rather than sexual offences, even when there was no financial motive.[4]

Between 1810 and 1812, a scandalous Scottish defamation case centred on allegations of lesbianism against two teachers at a girls' school in Edinburgh. The nature of the allegations was deemed so dangerous to public morality that the case was heard behind closed doors. Lord Meadowbank, the presiding judge, explained that 'The values, the comforts, and the freedom of domestic intercourse, mainly depend on the purity of female manners, and that, again, on the habits of intercourse remaining as they have been, free from suspicion.'[5] More than a century later, the case, which ruined the lives of the accused teachers despite their victory in court and on appeal, inspired Lillian Hellman to write her 1934 play *The Children's Hour*, which ran into its own troubles with the censors in Chicago, Boston and London when it was first performed, but is now considered a classic.

As recently as 1957, the Wolfenden Report on male homosexuality dismissed the idea of sex between women because 'female homosexuality made little cultural sense – how could two undesiring creatures instigate sexual activity between themselves?'[6] Lesbianism was clearly thought best ignored. Erasure and invisibility are the opposite of tolerance and acceptance, and ironically the fact that sex between women was never explicitly criminalised in the UK meant that there was no opportunity for lesbians and feminists to campaign together and build solidarity.

The criminalisation of lesbians is, however, on the rise in a number of countries. In some former British colonies, the 1922 law of gross indecency within the Criminal Law Amendment Act is still in place, in various guises. This law raised the age of consent for indecent assault (all sexual touching except sexual intercourse) to 16. It primarily targeted men, but included a section that addressed gross indecency between women. As I write, in June 2024, there are 40 countries around the world that criminalise private, consensual sexual activity between women using laws against 'lesbianism', 'sexual relations with a person of the same sex' and 'gross indecency'.

In the UK, the Equality Act of 2010 made discrimination against lesbians (and gay men), on the basis of sexual orientation, unlawful. Since then, we have had formal legal equality. We do not, however, have social equality. Not with heterosexuals, and not with gay men.

## Have things changed for the better for lesbians worldwide?

Lesbians in the UK have fought for, and achieved, legislative equality with heterosexuals. We can marry, adopt and foster children, and have next-of-kin rights with a same-sex partner. It is illegal to fire us from our jobs or refuse us goods and services on the grounds of our sexual orientation. These rights are also widespread across the majority of states in the US and in many other countries around the world. But there are still plenty of places where lesbian rights have either been rolled back, such as in Russia under Vladimir Putin, or where, under the influence of religious fundamentalists, archaic and extremely punitive legislation has been introduced.

During my investigations into the prevalence of violence against lesbians, a senior UN official told me, at a meeting on sexual orientation and gender identity rights, 'We hear about the oppression of gay men and of trans people, but rarely do lesbians come anywhere near the top of the list, even when we are zoning in on LGBT rights.' In 2019, I decided I would visit Uganda, a country in East Africa whose government has passed some of the planet's most viciously discriminatory legislation on lesbian and gay rights. It offers a prime example both of institutionalised anti-lesbianism and of an amazing, awe-inspiringly brave response from the lesbian resistance.

In 2013, the Ugandan Parliament passed a bill that lengthened sentences for consensual homosexual sex and extended punishment to those 'promoting homosexuality'. It is illegal to be gay in most African countries, and in Uganda same-sex encounters can land a person in prison for an average of seven years. Same-sex marriage is of course illegal.

Freedom and Roam Uganda (FARUG), founded in 2003, was the first organisation in the country to focus on lesbians. During my visit I met Gloria, who joined FARUG in 2019. She explained what a struggle it has been to keep the organisation afloat in a country so openly hostile to lesbians.

Homophobic legislation in Uganda has its roots in the religious right of the United States. In 2009, American evangelist Scott Lively travelled to Uganda to set up an anti-gay movement, enlisting support from local preachers. 'The evangelists started the anti-gay movement and would go into churches preaching hate against LGBT persons. Before then, there was hate, but there wasn't a solid religious propaganda, so they started that movement,' explained Gloria. 'Pastor Ssempa [the founder of a community church at the University of Makerere, where Gloria was a student at the time] stands there one Sunday and says, "We're going to have a huge crusade that is aimed at fighting homosexuality in Uganda." During that crusade they were talking about how homosexuality is infiltrating the nation, and how white people have brought homosexuality here and how they are paying Ugandans to become homosexual.'

The result was a build-up of public hatred towards lesbians. 'We knew they were coming after us,' Gloria said. 'FARUG was struggling and had no money. I remember having an extraordinary meeting, and the person who is now our director stood up and said, "This is our child. If we do not stand, this organisation is going to fall, but I need you to understand that we started this movement. When I talk about the movement, it's not just about me, it's about you. It's not just us, the activists, it's the fact that you can still move in the street, that you can still access medical care, that we can still represent you in court when people are being terrible to you."'

I asked what specific problems lesbians face in Uganda. 'Initially, the women were oppressed just for being women,' said Simon Mpinga, the pastor at the Living Gospel World Mission church in Kawuga village, on the edge of Kampala. Mpinga also preaches at the Fellowship of Affirming Ministries church, known for its inclusion and acceptance of lesbians and gay men. I go to meet him with Nasiche, a lesbian who tells me she refuses to give up her faith 'just because of those pastors that hate us'. 'So, I think that lesbians are in double jeopardy,' says Mpinga. 'They are women and they are sexual minorities. Women are looked at as weak, they are unrecognised in society, especially in African society, because, when you look at the different religions here, they don't recognise women. They are not ordained as priests; they cannot be given the pulpit to speak about anything. So, if we want to advance the cause of women, we need to concentrate on the lesbians.'

A woman named Namazzi and I got talking at the FARUG Friday social. 'When I told my best friend [that I am a lesbian], the first thing she said was, "You are beautiful. Are you telling me there are no men out there who want to be in a relationship with you, so you decided to go and have a relationship with girls?" So, I told her, "No, it's because I want girls; the men are there, but I want girls." We are still friends, but not best friends any more.'

Very few of the coming-out stories I heard at FARUG were positive. 'I have lost some of my family members,' Lailah told me. 'Some don't talk to me; some don't understand me. At Christmas, you're expected to go to the village and be with your family, but they say, "That one, she's gay." So, I don't go home. I call and talk to them, but it's really hard. I miss them.'

Annise was sitting on the floor of the courtyard drinking a beer, her baseball cap pulled low over her face. 'My friend was in an abusive marriage, and her husband thought she was a lesbian with her best friend,' she told me. 'When she ran away from the marriage and the abuse, the husband followed her to her friend's house because he thought they were lovers. He tried to attack them and keeps threatening to kill them.'

The women at FARUG constantly spoke about police brutality. 'Some friends and I were listening to music and drinking at a bar when the police suddenly arrived,' Hope recounted. 'I saw some people jump over a wall to escape the beatings, and others hid in the toilets. Those of us who were left were ordered to stand in a corner. The police then marched us slowly all the way to the police station.'

Grace, a 30-year-old feminist activist and proud lesbian, approached me at FARUG and told me that she is 'sick of gay men and trans women demanding all the attention from the international community. We are the mothers of the movement; we are the ones to start the revolution. We have less representation. We don't have the faces and voices out there to amplify our issues the way we need them to. I don't know if it's because we're shy and most of us are in the closet. We have less of a profile.'

As I was saying my goodbyes, shouting over the loud reggae music, one of the young women, proudly embracing her girlfriend, told me, 'This movement is not going to end. We are getting bigger; we are getting stronger. Lesbians are strong.' But many lesbians have fled to a refugee camp in Kenya called Kakuma. When I spoke to a group of them over an unstable Zoom connection, they explained that they were housed in their own block, making them easily identifiable to others in the camp who then harass them, and worse. I asked them why Ugandan men were so violent towards lesbians, and one woman said, 'They can't take care of us, and they can't love in the way we want. We would rather love our fellow women. So they get angry. In Uganda, we are still having these old traditions that the man is always higher [status] than the women.' The other women were nodding along and shouting '*Yes!*' into the camera.

Ugandan lesbians are not alone in experiencing the type of hyper-misogynistic violence I heard about on my visit there. A report entitled 'Dossier on the Killing of Lesbians in Brazil', compiled by the Research Group on the Killing of Lesbians – The Untold Stories,[7] an association that gathers data and stories about victims of crime, shows that from 2000 to 2017, 180 lesbians were reported murdered, of whom 126 were killed between 2014 and 2017.

'Lesbophobia isn't just an act of specific violence that can occur at any given moment,' says Milena Peres, a 25-year-old lesbian and member of the research group, which also compiles data on suicide among lesbians, referred to as 'lesbocide'. 'What we suffer from also defines us. We are isolated, discredited, made invisible, attacked and violated in the most diverse ways every single day. Death lurks around us, as does mental illness, profound isolation and systematic devaluation.'

Brazil is marked by profound social and cultural inequalities, and I was told by those I interviewed that to be a lesbian in the northern region was very different from being a lesbian in the south. And white lesbians have very different experiences from black, quilombola or indigenous lesbians. 'The lesbian invisibility is expressed through the systemic annihilation and denial of the lesbian existence, of the disparagement and creation of myths about us which do not speak truth to who we are and how we live,' Peres said. 'When we are murdered, our deaths aren't accurately disclosed, and our memories are disrespected.'

Across Iran, women's rights, freedom of movement and freedom of expression are extremely restricted, and the strict patriarchal structure allows fathers, brothers and husbands to exercise direct control over women and girls. For lesbians, life is especially difficult. 'Being Lesbian in Iran',[8] a report by the human rights campaign group OutRight Action International, stated that 'Lesbian community members in the Islamic Republic of Iran are subjected to a confluence of legal discrimination, social harassment, domestic abuse, and acts of violence, inflicted by both state officials and private citizens.' Violence and abuse is endemic. The following stories from the report offer just a couple of examples of the state-sponsored trauma and punishment experienced by lesbians in Iran. Maryam A., a lesbian from Tehran, was forced to marry her 36-year-old first cousin when she was a child of 14. Faced with her fear and revulsion, he became abusive and forced her to see a doctor to 'cure' her lack of sexual interest. The medication she was given made Maryam very depressed. After years of abuse, violence and marital rape, Maryam did manage to get a divorce. She began a relationship with Sara, although she could only see her in secret. At one point, Sara contemplated undergoing sex reassignment surgery so that she could live with Maryam legally. In the end, the couple decided to run away to a small town in northern Iran – where, in response to a neighbour's complaint about the two women living together, police raided their home and arrested them. They were held in detention, separately, for several days, and pressured to confess the nature of their relationship. Following a 30-minute trial based on their forced confessions, Maryam and Sara were each sentenced to 100 lashes and a prison sentence of ten months. Maryam said that both she and her partner were flogged on the first day of their imprisonment. They suffered intense physical and psychological trauma as a result.

Azadeh, in her twenties, is from northern Iran. She was reported because of her sexual orientation to the Intelligence Office by her own father, a decorated military general. She was abducted and forced to undergo a 'reorientation course' and violent interrogation. 'The interrogators tortured me by pouring boiling water on my skin and beating me, especially on the head,' she said. 'As well as physical torture, I was subjected to constant verbal abuse. They kept telling me that I was a "pussy licker".'

Meanwhile, in Nigeria's Kano State, a 2014 amendment to the penal code created a new offence of lesbianism, punishable by up to 14 years' imprisonment. The Islamic penal code provides for a penalty of 100 lashes or, for a fourth conviction, death. In Yemen, premeditated sex between women carries a penalty of up to three years' imprisonment.

These stories serve to show how lesbians worldwide suffer violence and sexual assault by individual men and by the state, in the form of imprisonment, corrective rape, medical interventions and conversion therapy; they also suffer from the intolerant and archaic attitudes which characterise the response of many in their communities. Some countries have made lesbianism illegal by amending existing legislation on sexual behaviour; others have criminalised lesbian relationships via sharia law. Which leads us to the question: is there anywhere in the world we are free to live our lives in peace and safety? Even in the UK, where lesbians enjoy a level of legal protection undreamt of in some countries, lesbians are in danger. In 2018, in my home city of London, two lesbians were badly beaten up on a bus by a group of men when they refused their demand to kiss in front of them. The image of the bloodied, distressed young women attracted international media attention. A year later, in Walsall Garth, a town toward the north of England, 18-year-old Ellie-Mae Mulholland was beaten by a gang of men. She was told, 'You and your girlfriend are going to get it ten times worse next time.' The experience of violence at the hands of random male strangers is commonplace.

## Old forms of bigotry, new forms of punishment

Hatred of lesbians is a result of patriarchal attitudes that demand subservience and capitulation to men. Our very existence is an affront to bigoted, misogynistic men. Additionally, women being out lesbians can be seen as an act of provocation, even, on occasion, by those tasked to uphold the law and seek justice. When I was attacked by members of Combat 18 in a Leeds nightclub in 1981, I was laughed at by police when they realised I was a lesbian (due to a slogan on my T-shirt), and, to paraphrase, asked, 'What did you expect?' A more recent form of anti-lesbianism has emerged in the controversial area of sex by deception.

Georgia,[9] a lesbian, was raped in early 2018 when she was a student. During a night out with friends, she had got chatting with Sophie,[10] who later went on with them to a lesbian nightclub. At the end of the evening, Sophie seemed not to know where she lived, appearing quite drunk and somewhat disorientated, so Georgia invited her back to her place. Once home, they began, in Georgia's words, 'making out'. And then she suddenly realised that Sophie was, in fact, a man. Shocked and very upset, Georgia made it clear that she didn't want to carry on. Sophie then held her down and raped her. Sophie 'passed very well' as a woman, according to Georgia.

When the case went to court Sophie, as the defendant, chose to present in a fairly traditional male way. The defence strategy was to claim that Georgia was well aware that Sophie was a trans woman, and it was in fact her transphobia that had led her to make a false accusation of rape when she subsequently regretted the sex. If the members of the jury were unconvinced that the defendant could pass as a woman, Georgia must have consented, and therefore – no rape. Sophie was acquitted.

'Sophie gave no indication that she was trans,' Georgia said. 'You don't get to use your femininity to gain the trust of a female and then use your masculinity to destroy her. I felt and still do feel an extra sense of violation, at being accused of being transphobic in court after being brave enough to speak my truth as a victim of rape.'

Georgia's allegation of rape was in simplicity about her not consenting to sex with a penis and being forced into it against her wishes, yet the focus of the case became about her alleged transphobia. Georgia's mother got in touch with me to ask for advice after the trial finished. Her view was that had the prosecution focused on Sophie's deception of Georgia then this would have been at the forefront of the jury's thinking when considering whether an offence had taken place.

In contrast to Georgia's case, there have been a series of cases over the last few years where young women who were either lesbians or exploring their gender identity have been convicted and imprisoned for rape on the basis that they deceived the other woman as to their biological sex.

The Court of Appeal considered the question of whether deceit as to biological sex can vitiate consent so as to amount to assault by penetration in the case of *R v. McNally* in 2013. Justine McNally was just 13 when she met a girl one year younger on an online gaming site. McNally used a male avatar by the name of Scott. Over three and a half years, the two developed an online relationship, which became sexual. They met for the first time when the younger girl, 'M', had just turned 16. McNally presented as a boy, consistent with her online identity Scott, and wore a dildo underneath her trousers. Over the next few months, they met up on four occasions and engaged in sexual intimacy. On the fourth visit, M's mother confronted McNally about 'really being a girl' and made a complaint to McNally's school. The police were notified. M said she was heterosexual and would not have engaged in sexual activity with 'Scott' if she had known that McNally was a girl.

In 2012, McNally pleaded guilty to six counts of sexual assault by penetration. She was sentenced to three years' imprisonment. The Court of Appeal upheld her conviction, although reduced the sentence to nine months and a suspension for two years. However, with her convictions, McNally remains on the sex offenders register.

Following this case, a series of other cases have led to convictions of young women for deceiving others as to their biological sex. Many of those cases are disturbing because the victims were often underage, indicating grooming. However, one case that stands out is that of Gayle Newland, aged 27, who was convicted of having sex with a woman her own age with whom she was in a relationship, but posing as a man. She apparently persuaded her girlfriend to be blindfolded each time they had sex and used a prosthetic penis. Eventually the deceit was discovered when the woman removed her blindfold. The judge sentenced Newland to eight years (reduced on appeal to six and a half), commenting, 'It is difficult to conceive of a deceit so degrading or so damaging for the victim upon its discovery.'

Interestingly, the cause of these women has been adopted as representing miscarriages of justice by organisations promoting trans rights. Gendered Intelligence and Mermaids (both of which we will meet in the next chapter) argue that assault or rape via *deception as to sex* should not be treated as a crime. Stonewall has long been calling for a change to the so-called 'sex by deception' law, so that trans-identified men and women initiating a sexual encounter would be protected from sexual assault charges, even when actively and falsely claiming to be the opposite sex. Stonewall considers this a matter of 'privacy':

'Recent "sex by deception" cases involving trans people and gender identity issues have revealed an alarming lack of clarity around trans people's rights and obligations to disclose or not disclose their trans history to sexual partners. These cases demonstrate that it is possible for non-disclosure of a person's trans status to impair the validity of consent. This leaves a great many trans individuals at risk of prosecution for a criminal offence.'[11]

Stonewall fails to consider what this means for the privacy and safety of lesbians like Georgia who, as a lesbian, did not choose to have sex with a biological male. Nor would their concern extend to McNally or Newland who, it is understood, did not identify as trans but rather as lesbians, or perhaps were confused and hence hid behind a male identity.

In fact, the law around sex by deception is unclear and leads to other anomalies. In the case of *R (Monica) v. DPP*, the court was asked to consider whether the deception of a woman, 'Monica', by an undercover police officer posing as a political activist while spying on her and her network amounted to a criminal offence. The court concluded that deception as to identity did not amount to a crime, distinguishing it from the McNally-type deception which, it was said, amounted to a deception as to the sexual act. The Criminal Law Reform Now Network published a series of academic arguments on the subject,[12] arguing that the law required clarity and reform, although not in the form that Stonewall advocated.

## Fighting for survival

When silence and erasure are the methods of control, visibility is key to our resistance. But visibility alone is not enough. During that revealing debate in the House of Lords in 1921, Lord Desart, a Conservative peer, claimed that criminalising lesbian relationships would serve only to publicise their existence, a prospect that he found deeply alarming:

'How many people does one suppose really are so vile, so unbalanced, so neurotic, so decadent as to do this? You may say there are a number of them, but it would be, at most, an extremely small minority, and you are going to tell the whole world that there is such an offence, to bring it to the notice of women who have never heard of it, never thought of it, never dreamed of it. I think that is a very great mischief.'[13]

While the lesbian elimination strategy in 1921 was to suppress any mention of lesbianism in the hope that it might disappear, the strategy in 2024 is to expand the category of lesbian to include trans women, i.e. men, so that the term no longer describes a relationship between two women and becomes effectively meaningless. As I write, a media round-up of the Edinburgh Fringe Festival begins and ends with male comedians who both identify as trans women and as lesbians – one joking that he told his girlfriend he had something to tell her: 'Honey, it turns out you're gay.' No room for dissent here, and no room for the humourless ideologues who want to ask, what about that girlfriend, is she OK? And what about the female partners of women who suddenly declare themselves men, who are told they are no longer lesbians but heterosexual? The appearance of progress, coupled with the achievement of certain milestones in gaining rights for lesbians and gay men in the last few decades, can create the illusion of equality. But it all conceals a deeper threat to our existence. Rights are not irreversible, as we have seen with the overturning of the landmark *Roe v. Wade* US Supreme Court ruling which legalised abortion in every state. Threats continue to emerge, and old prejudices can be dressed in progressive clothing.

The latest form of misogyny comes from the people and groups who consider themselves progressive, including left-leaning students and graduates mainly under the age of 40 who consider themselves to be warriors for and 'allies' to trans people – at least on social media, where there is no danger of real debate. This lesbian hatred is all the more insidious and difficult to challenge because few people are willing to stand up for lesbians, and few people are willing to recognise that women's rights as a whole are at stake. Here in western Europe, we lesbians are fighting the biggest fight of our lives: a fight for our very existence.

# 4

# The Trans Trojan Horse Trots Into Town

Getting fucked is what makes you female because fucked is what a female is.

Andrea Long Chu, *Females*,[1] October 2019

I believe [Stonewall's trans rights agenda] is one of the most dangerous political and cultural movements we have seen in the west. It is an undemocratic and vicious movement. Most trans-identified men are heterosexual. Stonewall could not have failed to realise that extending the trans umbrella to include cross-dressers... was going to destroy lesbian rights and women's rights and boundaries.

Allison Bailey, black lesbian feminist barrister, 2021

On 17 May 2020, *PinkNews* published an article entitled 'The "gender critical" feminist movement is a cult that grooms, controls and abuses, according to a lesbian who managed to escape'. It purported to describe 'a dangerous, abusive cult, which pretends it is fighting for lesbians, but is, in fact, gaslighting them'.

The article was written by a female journalist who at the time identified as non-binary, and was based on an interview with Sadie,[2] a US-based lesbian who had been critical of gender ideology before doing a switcheroo to full-throttle trans activism. The article quoted Sadie as saying that an 'influential' British lesbian from the 'gender critical' cult 'even promised to find [her] a wife, so that she could stay in the UK and galvanise the struggling gender-critical movement here'.

Reader, the 'influential British lesbian' Sadie made these allegations about was me.

It all began innocently enough. An acquaintance, an academic at a reputable UK university, had been contacted by a young lesbian from the US who felt isolated and distressed. She couldn't find a community, she said, and really wanted to meet women in the UK, which she had heard described as 'TERF Island'. As a butch-presenting lesbian, she was constantly being asked when she intended to transition (i.e. become a trans man), and as my acquaintance had anticipated, I was sympathetic to her plight.

Sadie turned out to be very needy and vulnerable. She was, I soon learned, a fantasist who thrived on telling tales about other lesbians within the same social network – having her in your network was a bit like seeing a hand grenade rolling towards your feet. In the end, the visit never happened. She appeared to be offended that the lesbians she was in contact with about setting it up didn't have enough time to chat on WhatsApp, and she drifted away. Or so I assumed.

Unbeknown to me, a *PinkNews* journalist had seen tweets in which Sadie had poured scorn on me and others, and contacted her for an interview. It turned out that she had performed a massive U-turn and become a trans activist. She told this journalist exactly what she wanted to hear.

## The Trans Trojan Horse Trots Into Town

Heavily promoted on the *PinkNews* landing page as an 'exclusive' (trans activist Owen Jones shared it on social media as a 'must read' about the 'anti-trans cult'), the article focused on 'exposing' the lesbians that reject gender ideology. It was full of utterly outlandish claims, including allegations that 'lesbian journalists' who were 'household names' were overseeing an 'international network of powerful lesbians' that had 'groomed' many women. According to Sadie, she had been subjected to 'emotional and sexual abuse' at the hands of 'anti-trans lesbians', and the 'TERF movement' was shutting down any discussion of violence between lesbians.

Having endured almost 20 years of accusations of transphobia and bigotry from the so-called gay media, and particularly from *PinkNews* since its foundation in 2005, I had always thought it best to ignore them. But this time I had been pushed too far. The article was clearly defamatory, and the magazine's attacks on me and others who criticised trans ideology had become increasingly deranged. I had been a long-time critic of powerful rich people using the UK's strict libel laws to silence people, and so I thought very carefully before taking legal action. But I realised that unless I took a stand, this misogynist rag would continue to publish whatever it liked about lesbians who spoke out against gender ideology, and the personal attacks on me would never stop. If they were willing to repeat allegations that lesbians they labelled 'transphobic' had sexually and emotionally abused a young, vulnerable lesbian, then they would stop at nothing. As is well documented, I have spent my whole adult life fighting for victims of these kinds of abuse. I decided to sue.

After 18 months of litigation, I agreed to settle. They removed the article, and we issued a joint statement.[3] I continued to speak out against *PinkNews* – the only aspect of the case I had agreed to keep confidential was the terms of the actual settlement. I wrote an article about the case, sharing Owen Jones's 'must read' tweet,[4] and a few people, several of whom had themselves been seriously misrepresented by the magazine,[5] posted about it on social media.

Just days later, my solicitors received a letter from lawyers acting for *PinkNews*. 'As you might expect, our clients were disappointed to read your client's comments, particularly where they detailed confidential communications between the parties.' Of course, nothing in my article or tweets was 'confidential'; I would never have agreed to being gagged on the details of the case. So I decided to tweet the joint statement, with the heading 'I sued *PinkNews*', on an almost daily basis for some months. Interestingly, we didn't hear from those lawyers again.

◆

## All women need single-sex spaces

Having access to female-only spaces makes a significant difference to women's lives. As a young lesbian, I would never have been able to come out and be proud of my sexuality had I not been able to discuss my fears, prejudices and critical personal and political questions with other lesbians, including within groups set up for that very purpose.

Before I had ever met any feminists or come out as a lesbian, I was raped by an older man. I had no way of understanding what had happened to me and why, and of course I internalised the trauma. I had known for ever that I was a lesbian, but even so I wondered if my sexuality was somehow due to the rape. Then, after I had started hanging out with feminists and, thanks to them, coming out, I was attacked by two men at work, who were affronted that I was not sexually available to them. I walked out of that job and immediately told my lesbian feminist friends about the assault, who were as angry as I was. The difference between how I felt after the previous attack and after this one was like that between night and day.

This is only one illustration of why women-only spaces are vitally important and why we must fight to keep them. Without them, there is nowhere in the public sphere for women to air the difficulties of their everyday struggles with men and the patriarchy. Women talking among themselves can lead to the development of a feminist consciousness and the drawing of political conclusions. Campaigns are formulated, alliances consolidated, solidarity established and vital support networks built. If all of this discussion and debate is by necessity confined to private conversations between friends, it is much less likely to translate into wider political action. While the crucial feminist insight that 'the personal is political' might still emerge, the private sphere of female friendship is more likely to serve as a coping mechanism which enables women to survive in unhappy, difficult or dangerous relationships with men, rather than radically transforming these situations, or leaving them altogether.

Of course, lesbians live in the world of everyday sexism and face struggles in their relationships with the men in our lives too – at work, in the family, and in our friendship networks – but our lesbian women-only spaces are particularly precious. We need them to get away from those who consider same-sex attraction among women distasteful, of course. But for us, these spaces are the haven in which we construct our lives, meet our partners, socialise with like-minded lesbians, relax, dance, have a good time – and plan our next campaigning moves. And now that men have been admitted, in the name of 'inclusivity', these aspects of our lives have been largely driven underground (or online), and for some lesbians they have disappeared altogether. Our lives are smaller, and our impact on the world and our visibility in it are compromised. The word 'lesbian' has yet again become not only contested, but also used by some gay men and trans activists as a synonym for 'Nazi' and 'bigot'. These are the insults thrown at us for seeking out our own spaces and setting boundaries. And our enemies are not discerning. Lesbians are bound together by our refusal to adhere to the rules. Every out lesbian, whatever her views on politics or feminism, has challenged and/or defied sex stereotypes, as well as taken significant risk by being public about her sexuality, or simply not being in the closet. Whether we like it or not, lesbians are both a threat and a direct challenge to men's domination of women. If lesbians lose the right to single-sex spaces, we also lose the opportunity to shore up our resistance to new forms of repression and the ability to develop a strong social and political community.

As soon as the word 'woman' is interpreted as including some men, women-only spaces become mixed sex. Even if some women will still use them, whether out of desperation or in good faith, the spaces will inevitably cease to serve their most crucial functions. All women know that some conversations can happen only in the absence of men. And if we are no longer allowed to meet on our own, those conversations – about sex, abuse, men who violate us, our anxieties around them and our children, or indeed about our love for other women, or our desire to come out – will no longer be had. Perhaps that is what some people would like. But the removal of our spaces is one of the most damaging and dangerous consequences of the 'inclusive' language, now *de rigeur* in every 'progressive' circle, that has muddied the waters around the definition of a woman.

## Inclusive language as a strategy of exclusion

This past decade has seen an explosion of freshly invented 'identities' that confer specialness on even the least deviant of individuals. All you have to do to earn a place in the club is to question your sexuality (however inconsequentially) or decide you don't have any romantic or sexual feelings towards anyone else (which would make you an 'aromantic' or 'asexual') – the possibilities are endless. All of the above and more are now included in the ever-expanding LGBTQQIA2S+ umbrella – a collection of letters which does not represent anything resembling a 'community' and looks more like a WiFi code than anything else.[6]

It is clear that the once-familiar pairing of 'lesbian and gay' has long been obsolete, but the 'G' is for 'gay men' (though some lesbians describe themselves as gay); the 'B' is for 'bisexual' and the 'T' stands for 'trans-identified', or, as some would have it, 'trans'. The 'Q', standing for 'queer', is both exceptionally accommodating and slightly more edgy; it can be used to describe any of the above, or indeed someone who is straight but has an interesting haircut, but also a man who enjoys strangling women during sex, or any other 'kink'. There's often a second 'Q', which stands for 'questioning'; what this means is anyone's guess. The 'I' is for intersex,[7] and the 'A' (my standout favourite) is, as explained above, for 'asexual' or 'aromantic'. 2S means 'Two Spirit', a term used by some indigenous communities to mean indigenous and lesbian or gay – although in recent years, the term has been co-opted by trans activists to describe transgender individuals.[8] The final cheeky little flourish is a '+' sign or two, which is similarly open to interpretation. Maybe it is just there to keep any straight bloke who washes his car on a Sunday morning and plays golf from feeling left out.

First (and arguably least), the 'L' is, of course, for lesbian, which used to mean same-sex-attracted women of the female variety but which has been redefined by the gender Taliban to mean any self-identified woman (including the bepenised variety) who is attracted to women. In my old-fashioned way, I thought men attracted to women were commonly considered heterosexual, but here we are. Gender ideology, with its policing of language, means that the word lesbian ceases to describe a woman who is sexually attracted to other women. It has been appropriated by straight men, and we no longer have a word for ourselves. And now that we are all expected to be 'kind' and 'inclusive', a strong lesbian identity is somehow considered a bit 'off'; our pride and identity is subsumed by the holy rainbow.

This is not on. We need to stand firm against this form of erasure and embrace our lesbian identity.

# The Trans Trojan Horse Trots Into Town

## Holding on to the word 'lesbian'

When we, as lesbians, ask for help, support, funding – or even an acknowledgement that we are a group with our own distinct needs and priorities – we are now likely to be viewed with suspicion at best. At worst, the gender ideologues tell us we are bigots. The capitulation to this ideology by liberals and progressives has resulted in lesbians being viewed as 'transphobic' for simply using the descriptor of 'lesbian' rather than 'queer'. Why?

Lesbians (at least those of the feminist variety) are more likely than anyone else to raise our voices against any attack on female autonomy because we know what's at stake. A disproportionate number of us have been campaigning against male violence for decades. We were there at the beginning, when the Women's Liberation Movement was setting up refuges and rape crisis centres and fighting for the right to single-sex facilities and services. 'Leftist' men who disliked our agenda, with its focus on male violence, were at the time unable to deride us without appearing to be complete misogynists. But over the past two decades, something extraordinary has happened. They have found, in the 'trans rights' movement, a new and excitingly 'progressive' way to treat us with contempt.

## Lesbians are the canaries in the coal mine

The Trojan horse of 'trans rights' has charged into town, claiming to want nothing more than for men who identify as women to be allowed to live their lives in peace, and to be accepted as women without discrimination. Women who have raised the smallest question about this demand, never mind expressed any objection to it, have been pilloried as bigots and right-wingers, and plenty of people who should – and do – know better have gone along with this analysis. Some of these people are well aware that the movement is dressing up misogyny as human rights activism, but pretend, for whatever reason, to believe otherwise.

The onslaught on feminism has had a terrible, material effect on women in general and lesbians in particular. One of the most insidious and poisonous developments is that women who are same-sex-attracted, and especially those who present as butch, are today offered not the support they need to withstand the bullying, self-doubt and hatred that so many experience, but the option of social and medical transition so that they can 'live as' trans men.

When the trans rights movement first took hold a few years ago, the vast majority of same-sex-attracted young females being encouraged or enabled to go down the gender clinic route were from liberal upper-middle-class families in cities captured by organisations such as Stonewall (which formerly advocated for same-sex-attracted women and men), Mermaids (which campaigns for the 'right' of children to transition), Gendered Intelligence (which aims to 'increase understandings of gender diversity and improve the lives of trans people') and Allsorts (a Brighton-based organisation whose mission is to 'see a world where LGBT+ children and young people are free to be themselves'). But now it is not just girls from privileged backgrounds who are being encouraged via expensive therapeutic interventions down the trans route, supported by well-meaning liberal parents.

Figures obtained from the GIDS (Gender Identity Development Service) in Leeds found that in 2022, the highest number of referrals came not from London or Brighton but from the Lancashire town of Blackpool,[9] a place with notably high levels of child sexual abuse, neglect, poverty and drug abuse. Blackpool has the highest rates of poor mental health, suicide and serious self-harm anywhere in England. Girls and young women from all backgrounds are now being told that if they are attracted to other girls or fail to pass some random femininity test, they should become men. This is irrefutable evidence that women are under attack. If the category of woman is now represented by the contestants in *RuPaul's Drag Race*, then it is no wonder that lesbians who resist the stereotype of femininity are first in society's firing line. As I observed earlier, the treatment of lesbians is a litmus test for the level and virulence of a society's misogyny.

A straight line can be drawn from drag and the fetishisation of femininity to the perception of gender as performance, unconnected to the body. So it's both strange and disturbing that many trans-identified individuals assert that the body must nevertheless be altered to fit one's 'gender identity'. Gender, we are told, is 'in the brain', with the body a mere vessel that can be surgically manipulated into alignment with some kind of gendered soul. The butch-presenting lesbian is, according to this almost comically regressive belief system, a man trapped in a female body.

There is now a whole generation of young people seeking out diagnoses of body dysmorphia and willingly undergoing risky, painful surgery which will render them infertile and anorgasmic rather than accepting support and counselling which might help them feel more comfortable in their own skin. Why on earth has this happened? And why are young lesbians currently the fastest-growing group opting for cross-sex hormones and sex-change surgery?

It is a sad fact that the majority of girls and young women now presenting at gender clinics across the UK are same-sex-attracted. In Blackpool in 2023, I met Lisa, who told me she was hospitalised after she took an overdose having been raped by an older man. 'I was cutting, had been anorexic, and could not face what had happened to me,' she said. 'When I told the psychiatrist I hated my body, and could not cope with being gay on top of everything, she suggested I might be a trans man.'

So, this psychiatrist leapt to the conclusion that Lisa must 'really' be a man because she had suffered horrific sexual violence and had internalised her shame about her same-sex attraction. What do you call this? Because it looks to me like nothing but a new form of conversion therapy.

## Gender warriors versus lesbian battleaxes

Trans activists and their supporters argue that the rights of trans people trump those of women. We older lesbians are supposed meekly to accept that we are no longer allowed to organise any female-only public events, that we must include men who identify as lesbian women.

When right-wing men feel the urge to denounce or ignore us, they have no need to cloak their bigotry in progressive language. But the trans movement, while sharing this goal, does not want to align itself with the right. Conservatives approve of clearly defined gender roles, but somehow the trans rights movement must make its embrace of the same look progressive and left-wing. In truth, feminists and particularly lesbians offer the biggest challenge to gender norms. But for both the left and the right, a trans person is more acceptable than gay men or lesbians, such is their embrace, from different directions, of regressive stereotypes. The male left, having always had a tendency towards misogyny, has needed no encouragement to buy into the ideology that allowed them to express it and still be thought of as politically sound; many liberals convinced themselves that here was a new liberation movement. Of course, neither acknowledges the urgent threat posed by the trans movement to hard-won women's rights.

Any female born into a democratic society (outside of a deeply conservative or strictly observant religious community) in the past 30 years or so will have reaped the benefits of both the women's and the lesbian liberation movements. As we saw with Sam and Jen in Chapter 2, many young people consider their rights to have evolved organically, almost inevitably, and take them completely for granted. And because there are now very few decent feminist studies courses left in our educational institutions, they are often unaware of what actual grassroots feminist campaigning *is* – let alone how much it has achieved.

Many upper-middle-class progressives in their forties and fifties, at least those living in progressive-heavy places such as Brighton and some parts of north London, consider having a lesbian or gay child to be terribly old-fashioned, and seem to prefer their child to 'come out' as 'non-binary' or transgender. 'Affirming' one's child as 'trans' has become a progressive badge of honour for these enlightened parents. Others are genuinely at a loss as to how to respond to the new tyranny of pronouns and new forms of identity crisis among their teenage children, and feel, in some ways understandably, that the safest route is to go along with the gender ideology that is adopted not only by their child but by teachers and therapists and most other professionals to whom they turn for advice – because this approach has been adopted by countless public-sector institutions and individuals, including schools, universities, social services, family therapy services, GPs/clinicians and the NHS in general.

A parent who has 'affirmed' their child as 'trans' or 'non-binary' has taken only their first step. It is salutary to look, for example, at the case of the incredibly famous and popular actor David Tennant. He began by wearing a T-shirt at a film preview (obviously attended by paparazzi) emblazoned with the slogan 'Leave trans kids alone you absolute freaks'. But now he has gone all in. At the 2024 British LGBT Awards, where he accepted an award for being a 'Celebrity Ally', he gave a humble acceptance speech declaring that he was 'a little depressed' over getting an award for simply saying obvious facts like 'everyone has the right to be who they want to be and live their life how they want to live it as long as they're not hurting anyone'. He also expressed his wish that Kemi Badenoch, who was the Minister for Equalities in the Conservative government at the time, would 'not exist any more', and 'shut up', while claiming to wish her no ill. Badenoch, a young black woman and rising star in her party, responded robustly on X/Twitter: 'I will not shut up. I will not be silenced by men who prioritise applause from Stonewall over the safety of women and girls. A rich, lefty, white male celebrity so blinded by ideology he can't see the optics of attacking the only black woman in government by calling publicly for my existence to end…'[10] Later on in the evening, Tennant gave an interview during which he graciously accepted praise from the interviewer, describing those who disagree with him on trans issues as 'a tiny bunch of little whinging fuckers who are on the wrong side of history, and they'll all go away soon'. Kemi Badenoch is now the leader of the Conservative Party, which must be very upsetting for him.

Tennant is fairly representative of those trans activist parents who start off by standing up for the 'rights' of 'trans kids' and then progress to the whole 'trans women are women', 'trans men are men' and 'non-binary identities are valid' package. (I have to say, in all my decades of activism, I've never heard a less inspiring call to arms than that final non-binary flourish.) When people like him are asked about wholeheartedly embracing an ideology so wedded to gender stereotypes that its actual flag is pink and blue, or how they could possibly take the side of male sex offenders when they demand access to women's prisons, they just shrug and call us bigots. They tell us to be kind, and say it's more *nuanced* than that, or even that such trifling matters as housing rapists in women's prisons should be decided on a case-by-case basis. Prior to the trans takeover, none of them would have dreamt of arguing that men should be allowed into women's hospital wards, changing rooms or rape crisis centres on the basis of whether or not they liked or approved of each individual.

In recent years, lesbians have been told that we are not even welcome on online dating sites that are specifically *for* same-sex-attracted females unless we are willing to consider hooking up with one of the numerous men pretending to be not just women but lesbians on those sites. My friend Lucy Masoud, a lesbian in her forties, was kicked off Hinge (a dating app) and handed a lifetime ban for stating in her profile that she was interested only in 'biological females' because despite having set the app to 'women seeking women', every third or fourth match she was offered was a trans-identified male.

More notorious has been the ongoing case being fought by the Australian businesswoman Sall Grover, who in 2020 set up an app called Giggle, exclusively for women. On Giggle, women could find a flatmate, or organise social meet-ups. Lesbians were able to use it as a dating site. Grover came under attack as soon as activists, having noticed that the app was 'for females only', began demanding that Giggle be 'trans inclusive'. In 2021 she was sued by a trans-identified man named Roxanne Tickle who claimed to have been unlawfully prevented from using the app on the grounds that he was not a woman.

I met Grover when she visited London a couple of weeks before her case was due to be heard in April 2024 at the Federal Court in Sydney. She is warm and personable and possesses that essential quality for the fight against gender madness: a great sense of humour. She explained that the case would challenge the Australian government's ongoing attempt to banish 'woman', 'female' and 'girl' as sex-based categories. In *Tickle v. Giggle*, what was at stake was whether gender identity trumps biological sex. Grover rejected the offer of an out-of-court settlement conditional on her attendance at gender identity education sessions and her agreeing to open up the Giggle app to males. Her perseverance has come at a huge personal and financial cost.

## The Trans Trojan Horse Trots Into Town

The judgment was handed down in August 2024, 18 weeks after the hearing. According to Justice Robert Bromwich, case law has consistently found that sex is 'changeable and not necessarily binary'. In other words, women no longer exist as a separate category in Australia. Tickle was described in the judgment as a person 'whose sex is recognised by an official, updated, Queensland birth certificate' and Giggle and Grover were found to have indirectly discriminated against him.

This judgment, which to be fair only reflected the law as amended by Julia Gillard's government in 2013, effectively destroys single-sex spaces and services for Australian women and girls. It can now be argued that any female-only service, space or facility is discriminatory if it excludes trans-identified males. At the time of writing, Grover is preparing to take the case to Australia's Supreme Court. Tickle told the press after the case that he hoped the result would be 'healing for trans and gender-diverse people'. As Martina Navratilova quipped when she was a guest on The Lesbian Project podcast, it is indeed too bad Roxanne's name is not Tess.[11]

This has become a feature of lesbian life in the UK too. Even as I was working on this book, on 14 September 2024, Jenny Watson, a 32-year-old lesbian living in London, arrived at the She Bar in Soho shortly before 10pm. She was in a happy, relaxed mood, having earlier that evening hosted a fun event for lesbian and bisexual women who were able to meet without the presence of men, trans-identified or not, by constituting themselves as a private members' club. Jenny hadn't been to the She Bar for a while; she had been lying low since being branded a transphobic bigot a year previously when she had been organising and hosting regular successful lesbian speed-dating events at a pub in central London called the College Arms. There were usually between 30 and 40 attendees; two couples who met there are now married. But after a while, trans-identified men claiming to be lesbians started turning up. One evening, one such man, with a visible erection, sexually harassed a woman in the toilets, and Jenny barred him. In the aftermath of this incident, she added a line on the website making it clear that the evening was open to women only, the 'lesbian' descriptor apparently not making it sufficiently clear.

The perpetrator soon joined a trans activist WhatsApp group and began organising against Jenny. He contacted her employers, making allegations and demanding she lose her job. Activists targeted the venue, which had come under new management; the landlord posted on the WhatsApp group, 'Fucking fuckers if they are using my new pub they are fucking gone, TERFy assholes.' So far, so familiar. The College Arms cancelled all future speed-dating nights organised by Jenny and put out a statement that in the future, they would run 'more inclusive events', i.e. mixed-sex.

That evening at the She Bar, Jenny paid the entrance fee and saw, as she went down the stairs into the main area, a sign reading 'TERF free zone' and another proclaiming 'L with the T'. Jenny took a selfie with the signs. She noticed that there were bar staff and a couple of other men 'presenting' as female, but such men had become a feature of lesbian life by then, so she wasn't particularly surprised. There was also a big group of trans-identified men in a corner, and when she went to get a drink, one of them pushed his genitals against her. After his assault, Jenny hung out with two women, dancing and chatting, and avoided talking to or even looking at anyone else. But only an hour and a half after she had arrived, a female security staff member, soon joined by a man, asked her to step upstairs. Jenny followed her, and then realised that she was being thrown out; she surmised that the man who had pushed his groin into her had complained to the management, although when she asked for a reason for her ejection, they refused to say. She was handed her jacket with her house keys and phone in the pocket, and security used physical force to remove her from the premises, saying the venue was 'trans inclusive'. Her drink was knocked out of her hand. They tried to wrest her phone from her grasp, believing that she was filming them, but she managed to keep hold of it. Jenny was accused of inciting a hate crime – a baseless and ridiculous accusation.

Outside, Jenny flagged down two police officers and explained what had happened, but they were dismissive, saying that the management of any pub or club have the right to eject anyone. One of the officers told her that she must have made transphobic comments, because the staff said that she had. She was threatened with arrest if she attempted to go back in.

I spoke to Jenny soon afterwards, and she was shaken and traumatised by having been ejected with physical force from a so-called lesbian space because some trans-identified men took offence at her presence. Men such as these are punishing us for saying 'no' to them by attempting to destroy our spaces, our community and our wellbeing. But Jenny will not let this go. She is one of a growing number of younger women who are determined to recreate lesbian physical spaces. For this, she has been severely punished.

Lesbians have always known that setting boundaries is dangerous. It is when we say no to men that we are most at risk, and this is why so many lesbians cave in to the pressure to be 'trans inclusive'. But it now seems that men claiming to be lesbians have more rights than actual lesbians. Terrified of falling foul of discrimination law or being branded 'transphobic', organisations defer to the views of lobby groups like Stonewall. The result is discrimination and even violence against lesbians. Kemi Badenoch famously observed during a parliamentary debate that 'Stonewall does not make the law in this country',[12] thus incurring the displeasure of David Tennant. But what has happened to Jenny Watson illustrates that, given the way organisations and institutions behave, it might as well. It is the job of the lesbian resistance to reverse that.

## Anything BUT lesbian

At Glastonbury 2024 there was a lesbian tent; TV footage showed a load of young men nonchalantly strolling in to join their 'cisters' (as some put it). And we have already encountered, in Chapter 1, the 'lesbian' club in Hackney, La Camionera, where 'all genders', all sexualities and assorted allies are welcome. So: absolutely anyone.

While trans women and other males are being encouraged to call *them*selves lesbians, actual lesbians are being actively discouraged from calling *our*selves lesbians. Because lesbian is a great, cool word, right? But it's only great and cool because it has been wrenched so far from its original meaning – a woman who is sexually attracted to women. Now that they've got that pesky detail out of the way, the word is free to be cool. There is an analogy here with the way that decades ago a number of US political commentators described Bill Clinton as the 'first black president'. Why was Clinton, a white, Southern man, considered to be 'black' by those commentators? Because they relied on cheap and offensive stereotypes, such as the fact that he grew up in Arkansas (which was home to a sizeable African-American population), had black friends, played 'black' music on his saxophone, and liked junk food including fried chicken. When the story broke about his sexual relationship with White House intern Monica Lewinsky, he was compared to black leaders who had shagged around while married, such as Jesse Jackson and Martin Luther King, who were vilified for their behaviour. Clinton's behaviour, though, was cool and positive – because he was white. After his impeachment proceedings in 1998 and 1999, Clinton's rating reached its highest point at 73 per cent approval. He finished with a Gallup poll approval rating of 65 per cent, higher than that of every other departing president measured since Harry Truman.

The reason why the meaning of 'lesbian' and 'lesbianism' seems to be up for grabs is because many men, not just those that are trans identified, have imposed their own meaning on it in a variety of ways. Some assert that lesbianism is simply manhating; others that it only exists as a response to early sexual trauma; and, of course, it exists as a hugely popular porn genre. It is no wonder that some of us internalise all of the associated negativity and stereotypes. Feminism opened up the possibility that we could have sexual relationships with women if we so desired.

This opening up wasn't just about sexual opportunities – it was a way of reframing our identities as women, of, as Lynn Alderson says, 'thinking of ourselves in relation to women, rather than in relation to men – which is how the culture would have us think, as mothers and daughters and wives and girlfriends. Suddenly, it became possible for us to look at the world from the perspective of women, and as lesbians too.'

## Gaslighting lesbians

According to a YouGov UK poll of July 2022, 'Eighty-four per cent of cisgender [sic] lesbians, and bisexual women in particular, are likely to have positive feelings towards trans people, and 66–68% of those say their feelings are "very positive". This mirrors national polling which shows that women are generally more likely to hold pro-trans views than men.'[13]

My relationship with Stonewall was never exactly close, but I would occasionally go to an event they had organised and was friendly with a couple of members of staff. For example, when in the spring of 2010 Martina Navratilova was auctioning a visit to the commentary box at Wimbledon with her for a Stonewall fundraiser, I contacted Ruth Hunt,[14] then Stonewall's Director of Public Affairs, and asked if I could do an interview with her for the *Guardian*.[15] Hunt agreed, and facilitated the whole thing. And when my book on lesbian and gay culture (*Straight Expectations: What Does it Mean to be Gay Today?*) was published in 2014, despite the fact that I had criticised Stonewall for being complacent, conservative, and overly focused on issues affecting mainly wealthy gay men, Hunt defended me on social media, saying that my book was worth reading.

So Hunt and I were friendly enough. But when she invited me to meet her for a drink in April 2014, it was obvious it wasn't merely a social engagement – I knew she must want to talk business of some kind. I was intrigued. Over a gin martini for me and a pint of lager for her, Hunt assured me that were she to become Stonewall's CEO, gender identity would not be included as a category alongside lesbian, gay and bisexual. With hindsight, I think that knowing as she did my position on gender ideology, she wanted to avoid any public criticism from me during her campaign for the top job.

Ben Summerskill, the previous CEO, had resisted the addition of the 'T' to LGB in Stonewall's mission, recognising the fact that sexual identity and orientation were very different from gender identity. But when Hunt did take over from Summerskill that August, one of her first acts was to add the 'T'. In February 2015, she told a journalist that, following six months of face-to-face and online consultations with more than 700 trans-identified people, an apology was owed to them for 'harm that we have caused' by previously excluding them.[16] Stonewall's head of campaigns said it would take about 18 months for the charity to become 'fully trans-inclusive'.

An advisory board was appointed made up of those who had been most outspoken in their condemnation of Stonewall's omission of 'trans people' – and also, incidentally, of my being nominated for the charity's Journalism of the Year award back in 2008. Sarah Brown (a trans woman who had once invited a political opponent to 'Suck my pickled formaldehyde balls')[17] was appointed deputy chair of the Stonewall Trans Advisory Group (TAG). Back in 2009, he had also published a blog post (since deleted) in which he suggested that 'the smegma-like mixture of dead skin cells, gynaecological lube, stale urine... on the end of a dilation stent when a post-operative trans woman withdraws the stent after dilating her neovagina' be named 'Bindel'. It takes quite a twisted and misogynistic mind to come up with this kind of suggestion, but Stonewall completely ignored the targeted and profoundly sexist attack, despite my repeatedly highlighting it to Hunt. Aimee Challenor (a trans woman who was then the UK Green Party's equalities spokesperson)[18] was also a key member of the Stonewall TAG. Challenor had had to stand down from the race to become deputy leader of the Greens following the revelation that her father, David Challenor (currently serving a 22-year sentence for torturing and raping a ten-year-old girl) had served as Aimee's election agent in the 2017 general election and in the local elections in May 2019 – both of which came after his father's arrest. The initial TAG meeting, chaired by Hunt, was attended by a number of trans women,[19] some of whom had targeted and harassed me over the past decade. Hunt opened the meeting with an apology for previous mistakes made by Stonewall – such as my 2008 award nomination, which she said should have fallen at the first fence. This says a lot – about both Stonewall's disdain for the general public and its lack of respect for democratic principles (my nomination was the result of a public vote).

By adding the 'T' to the 'LGB', Hunt set off a chain of events that reverberated throughout the UK and beyond. Individuals with power and money behind them, such as the publisher and entrepreneur Linda Riley,[20] jumped on the trans gravy train. Riley, who I have known for some years, was a committed pro-lesbian activist. But when she saw that transgender issues and projects were attracting serious funding, she began to include trans-identified males as 'lesbians' in her publications, such as *Diva* magazine. At that stage, any lesbian with any kind of profile and public persona who didn't go all out to include trans-identifying people was told she was on 'the wrong side of history'.

## What pride?

During Pride (the Holy Month of) in June 2024, posters appeared around London, endorsed by the Mayor, Sadiq Khan, and supported by corporate sponsors including Tesco, depicting a young woman with a bare chest who identified as 'non-binary' and had clearly undergone a double mastectomy. Kate Barker, CEO of the LGB Alliance, wrote to Khan, describing the campaign as an attack on lesbians. 'Your campaign tells vulnerable young women, most of whom are simply coming to terms with their own orientation as lesbians, that it's "cool" to surgically remove their healthy breasts.'

I was initially hesitant to write anything here about the treatment of lesbians by transgender activists, partly so as not to attract the attention of the book-banning mob. But there is one particular story, about a very unpleasant experience I had in 2012 and which has been exploited by my opponents ever since, that I have been turning over in my mind, trying to decide whether to recount it here. In the end, I saw that here is exactly the place to tell it, because I need to explain how this horrendous attack on women's rights has affected so many of us on a deeply personal level. This isn't some kind of abstract fight; it has real, painful consequences for real, individual lesbians.

It began in 2011. The then-editor of *Diva*, Jane Czyzselska, and I were at an industry event, speaking about the outpouring of vitriol experienced by women who dared question gender ideology. Jane was trying, admirably hard, to adopt a middle position (I did say to her that this was about as possible as being a little bit pregnant). She could understand women's concern about trans women claiming to be actual women (my wording), but she explained that she thought that someone like Paris Lees – *Diva* contributor, journalist and trans woman – was 'genuinely who she says she is'. I suggested a discussion between Paris Lees and me as a way of exploring some of these issues.

Feminists have long understood that, unless you have a very high media profile (like that of, say, J. K. Rowling or Martina Navratilova), it is impossible to effect significant change as an individual; collective action is what is needed. At the time I instigated this conversation with Lees, I was feeling very isolated. I pride myself on my communication skills and ability to reach across divides and have conversations with people who vehemently disagree with me (and vice versa). As far as I am concerned, debate is the lifeblood of all feminism and indeed any politics of change. But – although I didn't admit this to myself at the time – my invitation to Lees was also an attempt at appeasement. I was worn down, exhausted, and looking to build bridges by the time I suggested the interview to Czyzselska. She told me she was appalled by the extreme trans activists and their demands, and she seemed positive about the prospect of some kind of peace process. By then I had already met with several trans activists to talk through the issues, including Stephen Whittle, a professor of equalities law, a trans man and a vocal trans-rights activist. In 2008, I had held my own in a public debate with Susan Stryker, an American trans woman and professor of gender and women's studies, at an event hosted by Whittle at the university where Whittle worked. By engaging in these debates, I had been trying to find a discursive and constructive way of moving things forward. More than anything, I wanted to get across the feminist perspective, which was up until then largely missing. People, including feminists, were very frightened of speaking up.

Around the time of the interview with Lees, I was beginning to admit to myself that trying to win the argument in the public arena was not paying off. I wasn't gaining any ground, and I was demoralised and depressed by the viciousness of some of the activists I had come across. The spotlight on me was unrelenting and was not helping to move opinion towards a recognition of the threat to women's rights posed by the trans lobby.

The set-up was pre-agreed: Lees and I would have a conversation which would be subsequently written up in the magazine by Lees. I knew it would be audio recorded, as this is standard journalism. I did not trust Lees and assumed he would pull a fast one by embedding audio clips within the article, so decided to also record it in order to protect myself against distortion and inaccuracy. There were no pre-agreed questions, and I assumed it would be a discussion about my writing and comments on transsexuality.

So, on the day that the debate with Lees was to happen, I turned up at the venue: the offices of a media company that published many gay male titles, including pornographic ones. My instincts were already telling me this was a mistake, but there was no way I was backing out. In the building there were a few gay men setting up the interview, and a video camera had been installed. I had not agreed to being filmed, but now found myself unable to refuse. I didn't want to be there. I didn't want it filmed. And the atmosphere in the room was making me uneasy, as the only woman present. To make matters worse, my voice recorder would not switch on.

My decision to go ahead despite my strong misgivings turned out to be a monumental error with consequences that affect me even now, 12 years later. It marked my last-ever attempt to participate in a pre-arranged dialogue with trans activists. Almost from the off, Lees was openly hostile, either staring at me in what seemed like an effort to intimidate me, or refusing to meet my eyes as I responded to his questions and accusations.

Lees went in on the suicide argument, asking how I felt knowing that droves of young trans people are taking their lives as a result of nasty women such as me. I pointed out to Lees that I was a 'gender-nonconforming' teenager, and that growing up as a lesbian on a rough housing estate was no fun. 'Looking at the definition used by many transgender people... I fit perfectly with that,' I said. There was no response. Things were not going at all well.

But the worst thing of all was that when Lees asked me if a trans woman could be a valid lesbian, I said, 'Yes.' He pushed further, asking whether two trans women in a relationship would, as far as I were concerned, be in a lesbian relationship. I am cringing as I write this, but I heard myself again saying 'yes', before muttering something about 'how a person identifies' and how I wished we lived in a world where we didn't have to have these labels. Shoot me now. I would understand.

The video and interview were published in *Meta* magazine, a publication devoted to gender ideology and culture, the following week, with much promotion from Lees and his friends at *PinkNews*. Because it was still the early days of feminist resistance to transactivism, very little pushback came my way – though I was, understandably, challenged on it by some of the more robust US-based radical feminists. But it gained traction over the years, and even today that interview is used against me by the single-issue women's rights crowd who like to yell 'Hold the line!' at me – as though I haven't spent the last twenty years doing just that.

This experience is also a clear illustration of how male power operates, how it is exercised, and how we as women experience it. In the above account I refer to Lees as 'he' – and this is particularly significant here. In my view, not doing so would mask the gendered nature of the experience, in much the same way that using the pronoun 'she' to refer to male sex offenders who identify as trans women masks the reality of male violence and distorts our perception of the crime that has been perpetrated (never mind the way it corrupts the data about crime statistics). His behaviour reflected the tactics of intimidation used by many men in the trans activist lobby, both then and now.

It took me a while to admit to myself that I had, in that interview, been the victim of bullying – and that that had been the case during the eight years leading up to it, ever since I had first spoken out against gender ideology in 2004. One of the myriad ways in which women are silenced is that we feel such complicated shame and humiliation at having been bullied, and tend to blame ourselves for it. Feminists are supposed to be strong and brave, which is translated to infallible. I have fought and won a fair share of battles against misogynists, as have all active feminists, but despite all my years of campaigning against the worst things men do to women, and supporting those at the very bottom of the heap, it turns out that sometimes the bullying gets to me, and I cave in, as I did with Lees.

As I was processing all this and wondering whether or not to include this humiliating tale in this book, I read a tweet by Helen Joyce, author of the bestselling *Trans: When Ideology Meets Reality* (2021), which described exactly what I had been feeling: 'I hate these forced apologies more than anything. I know several women who have made them, and the bullying in every case was so bad as to be life-changingly traumatising. They do more psychological damage than any other part of it. The woman always regrets making it. She loses self-respect and quite unfairly blames herself for being "weak". She ruminates fruitlessly. They're a humiliation ritual aimed at destroying her permanently and completely.'[21]

It's comforting on one level to find that I am not alone, but I am still angry and ashamed at having been intimidated into acquiescence. I can only imagine how much worse it was and still is for lesbians far more vulnerable than I.

## The last stand: lesbians under siege

In July 2024, trans activists protesting the Lesbian Pride March in Berlin were filmed chanting at the women marching, 'TERFs fuck off, nobody will miss you.'[22] Has 'lesbian' now become synonymous with 'TERF'?

The gender movement, in its elevation of 'gender identity' above biological sex, is explicit in its anti-lesbianism. It is also cynical and manipulative, deliberately pitting lesbians against one another. In 2018, some lesbians were persuaded that the right thing to do was head up a Pride March behind a huge banner reading 'Manchester Lesbians Stand By Your Trans'. Since then, the #StandByYourTrans slogan has been proudly promoted by many posturing, same-sex-attracted women who call themselves 'queer', 'trans masc', 'non-binary', etc. – anything but 'lesbian', which is judged to mean 'transphobe'.

When Kathleen and I were putting together potential names for The Lesbian Project Advisory Board, I invited a well-known older lesbian who, while not very 'political', has dedicated her life to lesbian culture and visibility. She emailed to decline, saying, 'What little energy I do have, I tend to use towards promoting intersectional dialogue within the rainbow community, rather than slicing it up into its bits… I wouldn't want to be associated with a project which, sadly, will inevitably be perceived as transphobic.' For her, it seemed to be enough that the project would be 'perceived' as transphobic. Enough, at any rate, for her not to want to be associated with it. This upset and depressed me significantly more than if a younger lesbian who had been involved in queer-identified politics had told me that both Kathleen Stock and I were anti-trans and that she wanted nothing to do with us. I would have disagreed with her, but I would have understood that it was coming from the indoctrinated culture in which she lived and operated. This was a salutary reminder of how far trans ideology had reached, even into those parts of our lives that we thought were safe from anti-lesbian propaganda, including those parts of the lesbian community resolutely untouched by feminism.

## Why all this matters

International Lesbian Day originated in the US, but in 2020, Linda Riley, by now a fully committed trans activist, decided that a single day to showcase lesbians was not enough, and launched Lesbian Visibility Week. In an article in *Advocate* magazine she wrote, 'I had noticed that more and more, the "L" in LGBTQ+ was becoming particularly marginalised.'

Indeed. I had also noticed this. I wondered what she thought about it. So I read on, as she proclaimed herself 'a proud cis lesbian and a proud trans ally', commenting sadly that many in 'the LGBTQ+ community' were beginning to equate cis lesbians with transphobes, and she wanted to demonstrate that this was fundamentally untrue. 'I wanted to help create a narrative that shows once and for all that the vast majority of cis lesbians are inclusive. We are intersectional. We want to remove any negative connotations associated with [the word lesbian].'

At last, Riley is talking my language, I thought. I too am sick and tired of lesbian becoming a dirty word again this past decade. But wait.

'So this is why during Lesbian Visibility Week we celebrate and centre all lesbians, both cis and trans,' she continued, 'while also showing solidarity with all LGBTQ+ women and non-binary people.'

I see. The 'negative connotations' are because some of us 'transphobes' exclude men from the lesbian club. We insist that lesbians are exclusively women. And Lesbian Visibility Week is for 'trans women' and any other 'gender identity' that feels an affinity with the label.

Riley is in good company with her comrades in queerland. Recently, UN Women (or Unwomen – sometimes the jokes write themselves) posted on X/Twitter, 'Remember, trans lesbians are lesbians too. Let's uplift and honour every expression of love and identity! Happy international lesbian day.' The strapline on its trans flag banner read: 'TRANS LESBIANS ARE LESBIANS'.[23]

That's us told.

The vast majority of people who attack, abuse and threaten lesbians are, of course, straight men. Now some of them appear to believe they can opt into a lesbian identity, despite their male privilege and almost always their male genitalia remaining intact (the latter fact seems to have escaped the notice of many of the 'be kind' crew, and it rarely gets mentioned when 'trans women' are being discussed). These attacks are part of a continuum of lesbians being told that we have no right to define ourselves or our boundaries. This is more insidious than attacks from old-fashioned bigots, because those who have bought into gender ideology and thus define themselves as progressive are incapable of understanding that their views are essentially rooted in anti-lesbian/woman hatred. And for the trans-identifying men in question, the concept of a lesbian is nothing but fodder for a sexual fantasy, and the fact that they have now been legitimised by UN Women is sickening.

Living as an out lesbian can be extremely difficult, even today. I recognise the bravery of out lesbians from the UK to Uganda and everywhere in between. But not everyone, including those who have reaped the benefits of the battles fought and won by lesbian/feminist activists, sometimes at huge personal cost, has chosen to put their heads above the parapet. And it is not usually because they are intimidated by a conservative, religious, violent, abusive or otherwise hostile atmosphere. It is because in many wealthy liberal circles it is now absolutely fine to say that unapologetic lesbians who do not believe in magic are bigots, 'transphobes' and – most unforgivable of all – out of touch with the 'new' thinking. Intimidation and silencing are the same, wherever they come from – and for those lesbians who do speak out about the men invading female- and lesbian-only spaces, the consequences can be horrible, and the misrepresentation of their views by trans activists will be almost surreal. But there is too much at stake to stay silent. We are witnessing the process of de-lesbianisation by progressives determined to school us into embracing the penis. How different is this, really, from men shouting 'All you need is a good fuck!'?

Questioning the centrality of the male erection in the achievement of sexual pleasure for women is still – astonishingly – controversial, but it is inconceivable that, prior to the march of gender ideology, anybody would have made the ludicrous argument that it could also hold true for lesbians. But now we are told that this is progressive thinking. The fact that the likes of Ruth

Hunt, Nancy Kelley and Linda Riley support this ideology is as shameful as it would once have been shocking.

## Women who don't have sex at all are queerer than lesbians

At London Pride, 2024, the march was led by Yasmin Benoit, a straight woman. Her oppression is, she claims, the consequence of her not wanting to have sex. As the 'asexual' ambassador for Stonewall, she describes herself as part of a 'community' that is 'invisible'.[24]

It might beggar belief, but asexuals, who would rather just have a cup of tea than have sex, have surged ahead of lesbians in the hierarchy of oppression. An asexual woman's oppression on the grounds of her 'sexual identity', i.e. not shagging anyone, is unlikely to have resulted in her being kicked out of her home, her job or her community. She is also unlikely to have been spat at in the street for it, or faced any of the other everyday stuff that still happens to lesbians today. But such minor considerations have not stopped Stonewall from producing a report on this tragically underserved 'community'. There is now an International Asexuality Day (6 April, for your diaries), to 'raise awareness' – because asexuality can include the demisexual, the grey-asexual and other 'ace' identities. And those corporations who love to demonstrate their progressive values should note that Ace Week takes place in October. According to Stonewall's report, 'Ace in the UK' (2023), the key thing about asexuality is that asexuals are not out at work.[25] From the point of view of lesbians who feel unable to be out at work and are therefore subjected to all sorts of assumptions about their sexuality, it's hard to see the problem. In fact, it is really difficult to appreciate the plight of people who want to watch telly rather than have sex. Maybe the asexuals should consider including those whose sexual oppression could best be described as 'being married'. And in any case, why does anyone need to tell their colleagues about their sex lives, ever? It's hard to see how *not* telling colleagues about *not* having sex can be a major issue.

## Trans ideology is a cloak for misogyny and anti-lesbian sentiment

Gender ideology is the biggest threat to lesbian liberation, and it's time to say so. It is part of the ongoing backlash against feminism and the renewed misogyny that blights the lives of all women. It has given misogynistic men – particularly those on the left – the opportunity to dismiss, patronise, and attempt to humiliate and control lesbians while still being seen as radicals. Talk about the wrong side of history.

Lesbians are a thorn in the side of sexist men and reactionary women. Gender ideology is a perfect cover for those who, while not wishing to appear anti-lesbian or woman-hating, have never been true allies in our liberation struggle. People like this will not be won round by reasoned argument. What we need is for our erstwhile allies to wake up and realise what is at stake. The trans movement does not advocate for a vulnerable minority.

## The Trans Trojan Horse Trots Into Town

We also urgently need male allies who can see exactly what's going on. And, thankfully, some gay men are now speaking out. A new and meaningful alliance is at last being forged between lesbians and gay men – and not before time.

# 5

# Brothers in Arms

> As we cannot carry out this revolutionary change alone… we will work to form a strategic alliance with the Women's Liberation Movement… In order to build this alliance, the brothers in gay liberation will have to be prepared to sacrifice that degree of male chauvinism and male privilege that they still all possess.
>
> Gay Liberation Front (GLF) Manifesto, 1970

> They [lesbians] should have been dragged off by their saggy tits.
>
> Male organiser of Manchester Pride, in response to lesbian protesters carrying banners reading 'Lesbians don't have dicks', 2018[1]

In 2001, I was asked by *Guardian* features editor Kath Viner (who as described in Chapter 2 would come to my defence three years later when my article 'Gender Benders Beware' was attacked by trans activists) to stand in for the provocative, rather brilliant writer Julie Burchill and cover her column in the *Guardian Weekend* magazine[2] while she was off creating havoc in Tenerife. I wasn't yet a journalist, but I had plenty to say about sexuality, male violence and feminism.

The piece I wrote was headlined 'Gay men need to talk straight about paedophilia', and the strapline read: 'Rather than campaign on the age of consent, it might silence anti-gay bigots if some gay men spoke out against atrocities towards children.' I had long protested the terrible slur about gay men coming after your kids (it was an accusation levelled at lesbians too – as a teenager on my Darlington council estate, my babysitting jobs had mysteriously dried up once the neighbours found out that I shopped around the corner). But by the time I wrote this article, I had become increasingly frustrated and appalled at some of the child abuse apologism that passed for gay male culture – the depiction of prostituted young men as 'rent boys' and 'twinks', and predatory older men being referred to as 'chicken chasers'.

A few years earlier, Peter Tatchell, a long-standing gay activist and campaigner who more recently has become known for tying himself in knots over whether or not men can become women, had written about a 14-year-old boy called Lee who had been 'having sex' with men since the age of eight, and was, at the time he was interviewed, being abused through prostitution.[3] Tatchell wrote about this as though it was a story of sexual liberation, rather than one of sexual abuse. I was furious. In my article, I suggested that gay men should speak out against this normalisation and consequent eroticisation of the sexual abuse of boys by adult men. I raised the spectre of the Paedophile Information Exchange, a paedophile activist group founded in October 1974 which campaigned for the abolition of the age of consent. Before it was disbanded in 1984, it had been supported by a number of gay men who considered paedophiles an oppressed sexual minority. I also mentioned a book called *Paedophilia: The Radical Case*, which had been favourably reviewed by a number of gay publications. Even though this column was published before the advent of social media, I still came in for a huge amount of flak for it, mainly from gay men. I was accused of being homophobic, of feeding the fire, of suggesting that all gay men were paedophiles; I was told that I was to blame for anti-gay violence; I was even held responsible for the recent murder of a gay man in London. My critics flat-out denied that the eroticisation of sex with boys was in any way connected with child sexual abuse. I weathered the storm. Partly because most of my gay male friends agreed with me.

In my book *Straight Expectations* (2014), one chapter explored the debate about the development of individual sexual orientation. As discussed in Chapter 1, I do not believe in the existence of a gay gene – that we are simply 'born this way'. When Patrick Strudwick, a journalist completely wedded to the notion that one is born gay, interviewed me about it for the *Independent* newspaper,[4] he claimed that, in refusing to accept the 'born this way' theory, I was handing dangerous homophobes the excuse they needed to force us all on to gay conversion programmes.

I thought this a ridiculous argument. Extreme homophobes have no interest in how or why some people are same-sex-attracted, or in reprogramming our desires. And since when did we pander to bigots by saying 'we can't help it', which amounts to asking for forgiveness? Later on that year, when I debated Strudwick on stage at a live *Guardian* event,[5] I made my arguments, and interestingly, Stella Duffy – the lesbian novelist with whom I often fundamentally disagree about feminism and female sexuality – crept closer and closer to my point of view, as Strudwick became more and more vitriolic and, to my ears, sexist.

The event was packed, and the audience was lively and engaged, as was demonstrated during the Q&A at the end. Afterwards, I sat down at a table in the hall to sign copies of my book, and when I looked up was surprised and pleased to see a long queue, many of whom appeared to be gay men. As I signed, some of them did make it clear that they disagreed with my take on the gay gene question; others took the time to tell me that they had never really thought about whether or not they were 'born this way' – all they knew was that it was a mantra often repeated by so-called leaders of the gay 'community'. But what most of these men actually wanted to talk about was childhood sexual abuse and exploitation. 'I've really struggled with some of the stuff we see all the time on the gay scene,' a gay man in his thirties told me. 'I was sexually abused by a male relative when I was ten, but when I've tried to talk about it, I get some blokes saying things like, "Ooh, lucky you!" It's made me feel confused, and it stopped me from getting help for a long time.'

I stayed for quite a while, chatting to some of the gay men in the bar. 'If only I had known I could talk to lesbians about this stuff,' said Tom, a gay man in his early fifites. 'I had no idea we would connect on so many things.' Two days later, I received flowers from his partner, Jay, with a card attached: 'Thank you for saying the things we have needed to hear all these years. It feels like a cloud has lifted'.

◆

The first Gay Liberation Front (GLF) demonstration in Britain was held in Highbury Fields, north London, in November 1970. A then-nineteen-year-old Bev Jackson spoke to the press about why the group had been founded: 'It is important to know that we are not ashamed to be homosexual.' However, the majority of lesbians involved in the GLF in the UK left *en masse* in 1973 because they were sick of the sexism they were experiencing from many of the gay men involved. In 2019, Jackson 'came out of retirement' to set up the LGB Alliance because of the shocking *volte face* on gay rights she had witnessed from Stonewall.

I recently asked Jackson about her take on sexism within the GLF.

'I actually "emigrated" before most of the other lesbians,' she told me. 'I often quote a remark made by one chap at the second meeting – at which there were about 95 men and five women. He said: "We should invite Women's Liberation to one of our meetings." And another chap said, "Yes! They can bring sandwiches and coffee!" Loud laughter ensued. The memory of that laughter has haunted me, and I could immediately sense that working with men and women together would be a challenge, to put it mildly. Although many of the men involved in Gay Lib were very interested in promoting women's rights and gay rights in tandem, there was also a large misogynistic contingent. Since lesbians did not feel their concerns were being sufficiently represented, they split to form their own group.'

In 1977, the year I was outed as a lesbian at school aged 15, newly elected Labour MP Maureen Colquhoun came out as 'gay and proud of it'. But even though the visibility of the gay rights movement and the Women's Liberation Movement had by then achieved new heights, Colquhoun's constituency party voted to deselect her that September, citing 'her obsession with trivialities such as women's rights'. In the aftermath, local party chairman Norman Ashby said: 'She was elected as a working wife and mother... This business has blackened her image irredeemably.' The vote was overruled in 1978, but many in her party were unwilling to work with her, and she lost her seat in the Conservative landslide of 1979.

The next MP to come out as gay was Chris Smith, seven years later in 1984. No such vilification came his way – quite the reverse; his unscripted 'coming out' announcement at a gay rights rally was greeted with a standing ovation. Smith is regularly and infuriatingly lauded as the UK's 'first openly gay MP'.

Some might suggest that the different treatment received by Colquhoun and Smith is down to the seven years between the two coming out. But I would say it has less to do with the passage of time than with the fact that women are severely judged and punished – even more so than gay men – for defying orthodoxy. In other words, it is down to sexism. At that time, very few women were even elected to Parliament, and those that were tended to be seen as harridans for daring to step into public life. So Colquhoun, as a proud lesbian within this context, was a prime target for sexists.

One person who really understands the fact that lesbians do not operate on a level playing field with gay men is Gareth Roberts, columnist, author and TV scriptwriter. I asked him what he thinks of the way gender activists differentiate between the two groups.

'I'd always been aware of the "I'm a lesbian trapped in a man's body" joke made by some straight men,' he told me. 'When it started being said seriously, and accepted as true around the institutions, I thought I must be going mad. It couldn't be happening.' Roberts told me that he was 'jolted awake' by the late Magdalen Berns's YouTube videos in which she took apart gender ideology and associated misogyny with a caustic wit: 'She was saying what was in my mind, very directly and unafraid. It was so obviously wrong, and so obviously misogynist, that I couldn't – still can't – get my head around why it wasn't being laughed to scorn.'

For Roberts, the past decade has been an eye-opener. 'I just assumed that gay men would look at what was happening to lesbians and say "No" alongside them,' he says. 'But bog-standard male entitlement runs deeper than I thought. But I'm sensing that more gay men are stepping forward now, and to the scared ones I hear from, I say, "OK, if you speak out publicly it may well cause problems – but what you do is bung a tenner to the court case funds of the women being persecuted." That's another way of speaking up.'

Lesbians and gay men have been engaged in a protracted courtship for many years now. As we have seen, gay male interests, habits and practices had always tended to be largely separate and divergent from those of lesbians, if occasionally adjacent. The priorities for gay men tended to be laws against sex in public places, and the unequal age of consent. But in the 1980s, a set of adverse circumstances conspired to encourage lesbians and gay men to join forces.

In 1988, lesbians and gay men were both targeted by the same legislation for the first time, under Section 28 of the Local Government Act. Section 28 made it illegal for local authorities to 'promote homosexuality' in state schools, perpetuating the idea that same-sex relationships destroy traditional family values. The picture book *Jenny Lives With Eric and Martin* was found in an Inner London Education Authority Teachers' Centre, and a media storm ensued. The outcome was that most teachers came to believe that, under the new law, they were not even allowed to intervene in cases of anti-lesbian and gay bullying.

Around the same time, the HIV/AIDS crisis came as a bolt from the blue, bringing with it an unprecedented level of demonisation of gay and bisexual men. It had never been as bad as it was in the mid-80s – not even in the pre-Wolfenden days. An onslaught of blame and scapegoating was coming from politicians, the tabloid press and broad sections of the clergy. Between the early 1970s and the mid-80s, public attitudes had moved quite significantly towards support and acceptance of lesbian and gay people. The arrival of HIV quickly reversed that trend, and by the mid-to-late 1980s, two-thirds of British people polled said that homosexuality was 'always' or 'mostly' wrong. Many lesbians rallied round in support of their gay friends, and for the first time since the early days of the GLF the male and female strands of the movement came together. Section 28 created conditions propitious to bonding between lesbians and gay men; 'lesbian and gay' were yoked together, and Lesbian Strength marches merged with Gay Pride. But there remained significant differences between the approaches of lesbians and gay men towards campaigning against Section 28.

Gay men tended to argue that it was unfair to punish children who had been 'born gay' for something that was beyond either their choice or control. This argument was taken to its most extreme conclusion in a 1988 piece written by a gay man that appeared in the London listings magazine *City Limits*, entitled 'The Road to Auschwitz'. Obviously the title alone caused offence:

preventing teachers from discussing gay issues and identity in schools is bad, but it is not remotely the same as committing genocide. But still, it is worth exploring the author's argument, which was that gays, like Jews, cannot help the way they are born. Despite the outrageously inappropriate comparison with the Holocaust, the 'they can't help it' argument became the go-to line for many gay men.

The lesbian response to Section 28 was driven by feminism, which made it very different. While gay men were pleading for tolerance on the grounds that they meant no harm and were 'born this way', lesbians demanded respect and recognition, pulling a series of stunts designed to ensure that both the government and the public would take notice. In February 1988, three lesbians smuggled ropes into the public gallery in the House of Commons and abseiled into the chamber shouting: 'Lesbians are out!' In the kerfuffle that followed, several ushers attempted to apprehend the protesters – yet two of them managed to simply walk out of the chamber. And as I mentioned in Chapter 2, I was part of a gang that a month later locked ourselves into a model house at the Ideal Home Exhibition. It was Mother's Day, and our action mocked the idea, one of the underpinnings of Section 28, that lesbians were somehow not real mothers. One of the male security guards asked in puzzlement, as we occupied the house and shut the doors: 'How can lesbians be mothers?' We laughed, and someone shouted, 'There's a lesbian in every woman', as we unfurled a banner reading 'An ideal home has two lesbians in it and no men!' The day before Section 28 became law, four lesbians invaded the BBC studio in Shepherd's Bush during a TV broadcast of the *Six O'Clock News*. Their muffled shouts and thumps could be heard in the background as the presenter Nicholas Witchell tried to put his hand over one woman's mouth and prevent her from appearing on camera – an action which prompted the *Daily Mirror* headline 'Beeb Man Sits on Lesbian'. Those were days of protest and passion; lesbians were not pleading for tolerance or begging to be seen as 'normal'.

Lesbian feminist Claudia Clare was part of the Ideal Home action. She had been critical of the anti-Section 28 campaign's almost exclusive focus on gay men, and of their lack of solidarity with lesbians. 'One of the things that really pissed me off royally during the Clause 28 years was that there was a very particular attack on lesbian mothers, and that had a real, huge impact on them. And that was just not recognised.'

Lesbians and gay men were indeed united in their view that Section 28 was a threat to the education of same-sex-attracted young people who needed access to information to help them come to terms with their emerging sexuality, or of others who might be growing up with same-sex parents. But unlike many gay men, who were happily settling into domesticity, many lesbians were critical of the very concept of the heterosexual nuclear family, which they considered to have been constructed for the benefit of men. We were not keen on fighting for the right to be treated the same as straight couples and nuclear families. In fact, we agreed that yes, we were a threat to patriarchal structures, and revelled in pointing out that any woman could at any time choose to be a lesbian. For gay men, sameness and equality were indivisible. For lesbian feminists, equality and liberation were our goals; we did not want to be treated like men, and we did not want to be accepted as though we were just the same as heterosexuals.

Tensions between the two camps were building. I had once felt a great sense of solidarity in marching alongside other lesbians and gay men, but I had stopped going to Pride once the parade became dominated by roller-skating, cross-dressing nuns and leather queens. Not that there's any harm in a roller-skating nun or two – but the whole point of solidarity had been undercut by the theatre of gay male exhibitionism. Once again, we had the sense that the whole event – in terms of both its meaning and its performance – had been co-opted by gay men in support of their own agenda.

## Edgy lesbians versus cutting-edge feminism

For some lesbians, as well as gay men, there was a certain romance to holding 'sexual outlaw' status. But those of us whose focus was on challenging harmful sexual practices and their impact on women were profoundly uninterested in this kind of posturing.

Many lesbians had supported their gay male friends and allies in the fight against the grotesque bigotry and scaremongering of the 1980s, joining the fight for proper and dignified healthcare for AIDS victims, and volunteering alongside gay men at the hospices which cared for them. But while we might have come to be perceived as a single entity to the wider public, to the extent where an angry male bigot once told me he hoped I would get AIDS, that was far from the case. In the wake of the sisterly and selfless response by lesbian feminists to the attacks on gay men, identity politics reared its empty head – and with it, the whole agenda became even more senselessly anti-feminist.

## Lesbians

The early 1990s saw a growing number of lesbians taking up what had previously been seen as traditionally gay male attitudes on some issues, including the adoption of pro-pornography and pro-prostitution positions, engagement in campaigns aimed at repealing laws against sex in public ('cottaging'), and an embracing of S&M and bondage.[6] One case that illustrates the contradictions and splits in the various liberation movements is a notorious 1990 police investigation named 'Operation Spanner', which resulted in 16 gay men being given prison sentences of up to four and a half years, sometimes with accompanying fines, for engaging in consensual sadomasochistic activity which included scrotums being nailed to a wooden board, fisting, and branding and bloodletting. These convictions have since been upheld by the Court of Appeal and the Law Lords in the UK, as well as by the European Court of Human Rights in Strasbourg. The campaign against the police investigation and subsequent convictions was led by gay men – but it was also supported by a number of so-called 'pro-sex' lesbians.

The arguments put forward by the group on trial and their supporters were that it was perfectly possible to *consent* to assault occasioning actual bodily harm – and that the police, in picking on a group of gay male sadomasochists, were motivated by homophobia, which was probably, at least in part, true. But the divide between the lesbians who supported the Spanner men and the lesbian feminists could not have been clearer. By joining forces with those campaigning to decriminalise the perpetration of actual bodily harm on another individual during sex, they had shown whose side they were on.

It need hardly be said that most gay men didn't ever openly and directly support the feminist campaign, largely instigated by lesbians, to end male violence, including domestic abuse. And none of the lesbians busy anchoring themselves to gay men's struggles were actively involved in any of these campaigns. Their priorities were more about removing state interference from the consumption of hardcore pornography and sexual activity involving pain and torture. One of the key supporters of the Spanner defendants was a trans woman called Roz Kaveney – one of many trans women who have a sexual and political affinity with gay men, and who will speak up for men's 'rights' to use hardcore pornography and indulge in BDSM while ignoring or deprioritising the needs of women and accusing us of being 'anti-sex'. Kaveney was instrumental in persuading Liberty[7] to take up the Spanner case – rather controversially, because some people at Liberty were hostile to the idea and felt the men involved were beyond defending. But Kaveney was determined: 'I was the observer of the appeal court. And it was partly because of my getting Liberty involved that it got taken first of all to the House of Lords and then to the European Court [of Human Rights],' he explained in an interview in online magazine *Xtra*.[8]

Many feminists had a number of problems with the pro-Spanner argument. Abusive men in domestic and sexually violent relationships with women often coerce victims to say they 'consent' to the injuries inflicted on them by the perpetrator. Additionally, it is likely that a woman or a gay man living in fear of an abuser could be coerced into protecting him. And is it ever possible to consent to being seriously physically harmed, especially when there is an unequal power relationship between the two parties (which, feminists would argue, is always present in heterosexuality)? For us, the lines of defence were simply too close to those used to justify and/or cover up violence against women. The Spanner case was the catalyst for the development of a school of feminist thought about violence and consent; in 2018, the campaign group We Can't Consent to This[9] was founded in response to the increased use and acceptance of the 'rough sex defence' put forward by men accused of injuring or killing their partner during what they claimed was consensual sex which might involve choking or other dangerous and violent acts.

Following years of feminist campaigning, it was announced that this defence would be scrapped as part of the 2020 Domestic Abuse Bill. In 2021, I reported on the death of Sophie Moss, a 33-year-old mother of two who lived in my home town of Darlington, who died at the hands of Sam Pybus. He strangled her to death with such force that he told police his hands were 'hurting'. Pybus claimed she had died from consensual strangulation and had regularly encouraged him to do this. He admitted manslaughter and was sentenced to four years and eight months in prison. I interviewed his ex-wife Louise shortly after. She told me Pybus was violent to women and had tried to choke her during sex.[10] Other former partners of his gave similar testimony.

## A defendant cannot claim consent to serious injury

Feminist campaign group We Can't Consent to This focus on what they refer to as the 'normalisation of male violence'. Research conducted by this group found that between 1996 and 2016 there was a tenfold increase in rough sex defences used by men in cases where women had died.[11] Between November 2019 and March

2020, the defence was used 15 times. Back in 1990, pro-Spanner lesbians accused those of us voicing unease about the case of being 'anti-sex moralists allied with the right wing', even when information from the Metropolitan Police Obscene Publications Squad (OPS) suggested that some of the videos seized during Operation Spanner included records of abuse of a 16-year-old boy – and evidence emerged that some of the defendants were in possession of images of child abuse.

The merging of 'lesbian and gay' culture and politics led to both a growing anti-feminist backlash and to the so-called 'lesbian sex wars' of the late 1980s. Libertarian lesbians (some of whom had once called themselves feminists) began to believe that gay male culture, with its claims that pornography was great and so on, was more edgy and exciting than anything offered by lesbian culture at the time. Some took up S&M, donning black leather and chains; some started practising extreme body modification; others adopted the gender-neutral 'queer' label and began referring to themselves as 'sex positive'. The divisions between these lesbians and the campaigning lesbian feminists were detrimental and long-lasting. Damage was done both to the possibility of a common lesbian agenda and to the ideal of a radical politics of homosexuality that could have united all same-sex-attracted people, female and male. Lesbian feminists had hoped for a revolutionary political movement which would spell the end for a society based on patriarchal structures, but what we got instead was a movement towards a kind of equal-opportunities sex, reaching its apotheosis in the opening of clubs like the Torture Garden in 1990, which took fetishwear and BDSM mainstream and became a haunt for certain kinds of lesbians and gay men, and for straight people who liked to think of themselves as edgy and cool. This commodification of sex, coupled with the rampant individualism of the Thatcher years, meant that sexual liberation came to mean the freedom to have any kind of sex, rather than the right to a life free of sexual abuse, exploitation and oppression.

Also in 1990, four gay men, one of whom was Peter Tatchell, founded the organisation OutRage!, which described itself as 'a broad based group of queers committed to radical, non-violent direct action and civil disobedience to:

- ASSERT the dignity and human rights of queers;
- FIGHT homophobia, discrimination and violence directed against us;
- AFFIRM our right to sexual freedom, choice and self-determination'[12]

OutRage! staged its first direct action on 7 June 1990, at Hyde Park public toilets, to protest against the Metropolitan Police's entrapment of gay men cottaging.[13] The organisation's demands consisted primarily of the right to have sex without state interference.

By 1994, the gulf between lesbians and gay men within OutRage! had turned into open hostility, with some lesbians splitting off to form a chapter of Lesbian Avengers, a women-only direct action group initially set up in New York City in 1992. Its agenda could not have been more different from that of OutRage! Describing itself on the mission statement on its website[14] as 'a non-violent direct action group committed to raising lesbian visibility and fighting for our survival and our lives', it focused on equal immigration rights for lesbian partners, education, healthcare for lesbians and parenting and fostering rights. Another of its campaigning aims was to 'combat lesbian chic', which one of its members described as 'the male-ification of the lesbian aesthetic'. Lesbian chic emerged from the US in the early 1990s and was heavily promoted by the US media, soon spilling over into the UK. Magazines and newspapers ran colourful spreads featuring glamorous (supposed) lesbians sporting sharp men's suits, cufflinks and slicked-back hair, or ultra-feminine evening gowns and baroque jewellery. Many of us saw this era as a result of certain sections of the media looking for a new spin on lesbians, following the grim years of the AIDS epidemic and what seemed to be relentless bad news stories. But for many lesbian feminists at the time, 'lesbian chic' was a pornified male version of what lesbians look like.

As one lesbian told me at the time, the Avengers were appalled by male demands for easier ways to have sex in public, and access to younger boys to do it with, explaining that 'We were set up to assert the rights of lesbians to challenge gay male domination of the entire so-called queer movement.'

Two decades on, then, with the determined movement to depoliticise lesbianism and renewed enthusiasm for essentialist theories of sexuality, lesbians have, in a way, ended up back in the 1970s. And even now, gay men tend not to notice that lesbians' struggles are different from their own – or indeed even that women have been seriously oppressed. Gay men's interests often lie in upholding masculinity and prioritising their own sexual pleasure – quite different from the issues which motivate campaigning lesbian feminists. Gay men largely remain conspicuous by their absence in the struggle to defend lesbians against abuses such as punishment ('corrective') rape, and it is rare to see gay men speaking out *as* gay men about male sexual violence against women. Prostitution has, within some circles of gay men, been sanitised as 'rent boy' culture in which confident, good-looking young men seek out sex with rich older men for large amounts of money and attention and nobody gets hurt; pornography is a routine part of the aesthetic landscape within the gay male scene; and practices that feminists might describe as harmful and dangerous, such as the celebration of pain and humiliation, or 'BDSM', are portrayed as a harmless and even inevitable component of sexual desire. It is increasingly common to see almost any sexual practice, however extreme, described as a 'kink', and any criticism decried as 'kink-shaming'; dissenting lesbians continue to be accused of homophobia and depicted as anti-sex reactionaries.

## The surrogacy smokescreen

It is when it comes to advocating for surrogacy that gay men suddenly become highly visible.

Perhaps the reason lesbians are so at odds with gay men over this issue is precisely because men are men and women are women. In places where commercial surrogacy is legal, seen simply as a business transaction, from California and New York to Ukraine and Mexico, poor and desperate women are being treated as nothing more than wombs for rent – barely human at all. The surrogate mother is often required to sign an agreement which gives the 'commissioning parents' pretty much complete control over her life and body for the duration of the pregnancy. These women are left to deal alone with any postnatal health issues, and often find themselves settling for a far smaller fee than was originally agreed, especially when there are complications, or, obscenely, in the event of a miscarriage. Yet gay men seem happy to provide a smokescreen behind which the deeply problematic surrogacy trade can thrive.

In April 2022, married gay couple Corey Briskin and Nicholas Maggipinto filed a complaint against the City of New York, claiming they had been discriminated against because they could not access IVF (*in vitro* fertilisation) under the city's employee health insurance plan. Their argument was that, had they been a heterosexual or lesbian couple, they would have had access to these benefits. Under the plan, a person covered is eligible for such services only if they are considered infertile. This is defined as having been unable to conceive after 12 months of unprotected intercourse. The men said that this definition made it impossible for them to claim infertile status, and therefore they were victims of discrimination. Briskin told the *New York Times*, 'It's mind blowing that in 2022 we're still having this conversation about a policy that so clearly excludes gay men because of horribly antiquated views of homosexuality. We got the ability to get married and the rest would have been kind of smooth sailing, but we were sorely mistaken.'[15]

Given that neither of these men has a womb, it would of course have been impossible for them to receive IVF treatment. Their expectation was that they would be granted funding to rent a womb from a woman who would act as a surrogate. Claiming that they could not afford the surrogacy fees and multiple rounds of IVF (which they estimated could cost between US$150,000 and $200,000), they were seeking a change in the law and funding for the surrogacy services they wanted.

Lesbians and gay men (although primarily lesbians) had fought long and hard for the right for same-sex couples to adopt. But Briskin and Maggipinto have made it clear that adoption just won't do. 'It really feels like such an affront to be asked this question,' complained Briskin in another lengthy interview with the pair, this one in the *Guardian*. 'I find it deeply offensive. Nobody asks the person who's having children naturally why they did it instead of adopting.'[16]

I have not come across similar attitudes from women in same-sex relationships. It is true that many women who come out later in life already have children from previous heterosexual relationships and tend to be more concerned about losing custody of their children to their often abusive and violent ex-partners than with seeking to access commercial reproductive services. And prior to the hard-won legislative changes around adoption I saw many lesbian couples raising children together, while living with the fear that in the event of the biological mother dying the non-biological mother would have no legal rights as a parent. These stories are not given blanket coverage across the international media.

It is a strange twist indeed to see gay men promoting and propping up the surrogacy trade. High-profile gay men often show off their new offspring in the press and on social media – men like *Guardian* food columnist and restaurateur Yotam Ottolenghi, singer Elton John and Olympic diver Tom Daley. Countless non-famous gay men are following suit; it has become quite common on Instagram to see photographs of gay male couples in a hospital, with one of them, ludicrously, dressed in a hospital gown, propped up on pillows in a hospital bed, cradling a newborn, with the woman who actually gave birth neither seen nor mentioned.

Whenever I address this topic, in the UK or elsewhere, I am told that it would be homophobic and unfair to deny the right of gay men to use surrogacy services. And hardly any gay men, with a few honourable exceptions, have spoken out against it publicly. But a number of lesbians have been deeply offended by and concerned about the attitude of some gay men when it comes to their use of women's wombs and the subsequent discarding of the mother once she has handed over the baby.

Almost inevitably, gay male apologists for the surrogacy trade seek to excuse and justify it as a matter of a woman's 'choice' – a surrogate is painted as happy to go through nine months of pregnancy and the ordeal of childbirth in order to experience the joy of giving as she hands over her baby to two men. This narrative borrows heavily from the carefully crafted language used by apologists for the sex trade, the other business in which women's bodies are rented out. Supporters of the surrogacy trade are often also advocates for the legalisation of 'sex work'. Briskin actually made the connection explicit in the *Guardian* interview:

'I am pro-autonomy. I believe that people should be able to make decisions about their lives, their bodies. This is so relevant now, with the decision from the Supreme Court [the overturning of *Roe v. Wade*]. For me, it goes into the same category as sex work: there's this puritanical belief that sex workers are being forced to sell themselves. There are many, many sex workers who do not view their line of work that way.'

## That trans Trojan horse again...

Dr Az Hakeem is a psychiatrist who worked at London's Tavistock and Portman NHS Foundation Trust from 2005 to 2012. He explained to me his view that the transing of gender dysphoric children and young people is 'nothing but modern-day gay conversion therapy'. Hakeem means, of course, that encouraging children to alter physical sex characteristics, so that they magically become opposite-sex attracted, 'transes away the gay'. Organisations such as Stonewall have redefined same-sex attraction as 'same-gender' attraction, and in so doing have managed not only to remove support and advocacy from lesbians and gay men, but also to eradicate the concept of same-sex attraction.

Mermaids began in 1995 as a small group of parents of gender-nonconforming children who met to share experiences and support one another. Now it advocates for 'gender variant and transgender youth'. In June 2021, with the support of a coalition of LGBTQ+ organisations, it launched an appeal against the Charity Commission's decision to register the fledgling LGB Alliance (LGBA) as a charity. The LGBA is the only UK charity focused exclusively on same-sex-attracted people. I appreciate the need for such an organisation, and I see no reason why advocating for lesbians and gay men could ever constitute anything but a positive public service. But Mermaids claimed that the LGBA had been established to discredit and disband Mermaids, rather than to support lesbians, gay men and bisexuals. The LGBA's defence was that Mermaids had no standing to bring the case.

I was in court to hear John Nicolson MP, Deputy Chair of the All-Party Parliamentary Group on Global LGBT+ Rights, submit his evidence in support of Mermaids. He declared that, as a gay man, he knows what a lesbian is. 'You are a lesbian because you declare yourself one,' he proclaimed. What he meant was that male-bodied trans women are entitled to call themselves lesbians.

During cross-examination, Kate Harris, lifelong feminist and activist, one of the founders of the LGBA, was asked by counsel for Mermaids, Michael Gibbon KC, whether some people would understand that the word 'lesbian' could mean someone who is a woman as a result of gender reassignment. Harris broke down in tears, asking, 'That a lesbian can be a man with a penis?' Once she had composed herself, she responded: 'I'm going to speak for millions of lesbians around the world, who are lesbians because we love other women... We will not be erased and we will not have any man with a penis tell us he's a lesbian because he feels he is.'

The LGBA won this vexatious case, and it resulted in long-overdue scrutiny of Mermaids' own charitable status by the Charity Commission. In October 2024, it published its findings, declaring that Mermaids had been 'mismanaged' – which is one way of describing breast binders being sent to children without parental knowledge, let alone consent. The LGBA's legal fees were more than £250,000 – money that was raised from small individual donations. As Harris put it: 'while our win is great news for lesbians, gay men and bisexuals, we can't help but reflect on the fact that a sum like that would have been better spent on projects such as our helpline for young people, our LGB Archive and our Friends' Network.'[17]

The LGBA stands up for the rights of same-sex-attracted people; it upholds the definition of homosexuality as same-sex attraction; it understands the biological reality of sex. How have we got to a stage where this is seen by trans activists and their allies as hate-filled bigotry?

## Bonding between gay men and lesbians

The bonding between gay men and lesbians around Section 28 and AIDS, such as it was, came about in response to external threats which targeted gay men more than they did lesbians. Lesbians, while not typically exposed to HIV, did recognise homophobia when they saw it, understood instinctively that their gay brothers needed their help and support, and gave it unstintingly. Similarly, lesbians' experience of Section 28 was different from that of gay men. To many gay men, demonised for what was portrayed as their unboundaried sexual appetite, it was an existential threat; lesbians tended to be more sanguine. We knew it was stupid, we knew it was bigotry, we knew it was Thatcherism – but we didn't think it was the road to Auschwitz. But now, for the first time ever, in response to the threats posed by fast-encroaching queer theory and gender ideology, some lesbians and gay men have bonded over a feminist issue, one that is specifically about the removal of and threat to the rights of all women. Lesbians, as always, get a double dose of whatever is oppressing women – and that, in the current period, is gender ideology.

Dennis Kavanagh, a qualified barrister and legal commentator, is a founder of the Gay Men's Network, an advocacy group created in 2021 to represent the interests of gay men; it is rooted in the reality of being same-sex-attracted. I met him and his fellow directors Hassan Mamdani, a scientist, artist and writer, and Menno Kuijper, a Dutch copywriter, producer and brilliant satirist known as Mr Menno, whose gender-woo-busting YouTube videos have an avid following, because I wanted to find out what had motivated them to stick their necks out and support lesbians in a very public way as they have.

'We have recognised what is at stake,' Dennis told me. 'When we [lesbians and gay men] fought for our rights, we had to club together, and then we went our separate ways. But here we are again, this time joining forces to break free from the rainbow acronym.' All three of these men wanted me to know how important it is to them to have lesbian friends, and agreed that the reality and the seriousness of the present moment has thrown together people who mean business. 'When gay men and lesbians get together to sort things out, it's like a military operation,' Dennis says. 'And this is a very serious crisis. In these moments, we don't have a battle of the sexes.'

Of course, gender ideology affects gay men too, who are being told they should include trans men in their dating pool and welcome them into their spaces, and admonished that to describe themselves as same-sex-attracted is 'transphobic'. 'It's not just about our right to keep safe and be dignified with single-sex spaces,' said Menno. 'It's also about how it completely spoils our fun and means we are unable to relax if we are not just gay men or lesbians, either together or separately.'

These gay men believe that affirming lesbian and gay youth as 'transgender' rather than offering the support the young person might need in order to come to terms with their same-sex attraction is simply modern-day gay conversion therapy. And they realise that gender ideology's most pernicious effects are on lesbians. So for the first time, some gay men are prioritising lesbian needs, recognising the harm being done to us. Now, they are saying that if people want to come for the lesbians, they will have to come for gay men too. They are at last stepping up, and this is to be welcomed and celebrated.

# 6

# Lesbian Activism

> Until every woman is free to be a lesbian, no woman is free.
> 
> Lesbian Action for Visibility Aotearoa,[1] 2024[2]

> Fuck the patriarchy!
> 
> Martina Navratilova, message to FiLiA conference, 2023

My feminism is the battle for liberation, as opposed to its meek relative, the polite request for equality. I have no interest in playing nicely with the establishment, and I wish to disrupt the patriarchal status quo as opposed to becoming part of it. What is the point of that in a Britain where, to highlight just one shocking statistic, a mere 1 per cent of rapists reported to the police are convicted? Where the word 'choice' is more likely to be used to argue that 'sex work is work' than to advocate for legal, safe abortion? No society would permit the things that are still routinely happening to women to continue unless, at some level, it has contempt for us. If such atrocities were happening to men, the establishment would rush to fix things.

Lesbians face sexism on steroids, because anti-lesbianism is derived directly from sexism. This is why I argue that only by becoming active feminists can lesbians hope to achieve liberation.

Anti-gay prejudice (I try to avoid using words ending with 'phobia' unless I am describing an extreme, irrational fear of something that may cause a person to panic, as opposed to bigotry and prejudice) is also derived from sexism, in that gay men are punished for not being 'real men' because they are not keeping women in line within the heterosexual family structure – so surely it makes sense for them to join forces with feminists in fighting patriarchy?

But most gay men (and men in general) are not actively campaigning to end sexism and misogyny, and neither, for that matter, are lesbians. Many (but far from all) young lesbians take their rights for granted, have no knowledge of or even curiosity about the struggle it took to win them and the vigilance required to maintain them, and happily chant 'Stand by your trans' at Pride marches, prioritising the needs of men over their own.

What would it take to motivate *them* to fight for change?

## This madness *will* end

In October 2023, I was due to appear on a panel at the annual FiLiA conference which was being held in Glasgow. Just two days before the event, I got a call from Lisa-Marie Taylor, CEO of FiLiA, a campaigning charity which aims to build sisterhood and solidarity among women, locally, nationally and internationally; to amplify women's voices; and to defend women's human rights. The venue had cancelled on us. Fifteen hundred tickets had been sold, and three full days of events organised. It was, potentially, a disaster.

## Lesbian Activism

What had led up to this came as no surprise. Glasgow Trans Rally, an organisation set up solely to disrupt the conference, had been busy on social media. Because FiLiA advocates for female-only spaces, and the conference was to include discussions on sex-based injustice and male violence, GTR was encouraging 'trans allies' to target the venue and harass the organisers, both on social media and by phone. 'This weekend, a transphobic "women's rights" conference will be held at [venue],' read one of their Instagram posts. 'Prominent transphobes such as Joanna Cherry and Julie Bindel will be speaking, amongst many many others. STAND WITH US in telling [the venue] that Glasgow DOES NOT ACCEPT THIS, and that they MUST DROP THE EVENT!' And, with 36 hours' notice, the venue did just that.

Women were already on their way to Glasgow, some travelling great distances from places including India, East Africa and the Middle East. The sadistic narcissists of GTR were desperate to silence the voices due to be platformed at FiLiA, which included both survivors of male violence and lesbians. Taylor had already begun ringing round all the large hotels in the city in search of an alternative venue. She said to me, '*No way* is this event being cancelled.' She had also been in touch with the Joanna Cherry mentioned in the GTR post, that is, Joanna Cherry KC, lesbian, practising lawyer and at that time a Member of Parliament, who composed what was by all accounts a terrifying letter to the venue. The next morning, with 24 hours to go, the decision was reversed.

This kind of harassment has become absolutely standard at events where women gather to discuss issues that affect them.

## Lesbians

At a previous FiLiA conference, trans activists gathered outside brandishing placards reading 'Suck my dick you transphobic cunts' and then hammered on the windows of a room in which speakers were describing having being tortured and raped by police. I was in that room, having introduced my friend Zemzem, who was speaking about the sexual abuse she suffered during her journey from Eritrea to the UK, and while being held at Yarl's Wood Immigration Removal Centre.

Because of people like these, FiLiA has to have a security team at all its events. The team is very ably lesbian-led and is always a source of comfort, reassurance and humour; it is there to protect every woman who attends.

Arriving at the Glasgow venue early the following morning, I saw a very long queue of women waiting to register for the conference – and across the road from them, a crowd of young men and women waving trans flags and shouting the usual slogans. A formidable woman called Liane Timmermann, a regular part of the security team, calmly walked the length of the registration line, reassuring women that everything was under control. The sight and sound of mainly male activists shouting at the women, many of them lesbians, waiting to go into the venue to discuss male violence and oppression, told its own story. Suddenly, someone with a sound system started blasting out Tracy Chapman's 'Talkin' Bout a Revolution'. On hearing this anthem, written and sung by a lesbian artist, the security team started dancing, and soon hundreds of women in the queue joined in. It was a truly joyful spectacle, and an inspiring example of lesbian strength. The next day, as I entered the venue, two lone male protesters were sat on the kerb looking a bit lost. I allowed myself a little chuckle, gleeful in the knowledge that their mortal enemy, J. K. Rowling, would soon be joining me on the stage as a surprise guest speaker.

## Lesbian joy

I have already mentioned, in Chapter 1, Renate Klein's beautiful essay on her lesbian awakening, which I published on my Substack. She actually wrote it in response to my asking her, for this book, about her pride in being a lesbian and the happiness it has brought her. In her article, she talks about one of the biggest issues facing lesbians and feminists together: how we define and indeed celebrate choice in this most intimate aspect of our lives. How do we reconcile the fact that we experience our sexuality in ways so visceral that choice seems not to enter into it, and that given the difficulties we still encounter because of society's hostility towards us it might seem mad to choose lesbianism, while also not buying the argument that lesbianism is somehow innate? 'I don't use the world "choice" very often,' writes Klein, meaning that, as a feminist, she perfectly understands how women's 'choice' is so often curtailed and denied to the point where it is not really a choice at all, 'but I do use it to describe how I became a lesbian. I *chose* to be a lesbian and that was the best decision of my life.' Since discovering her attraction to women, Klein has never looked back, never felt an iota of sexual interest in men. She is just one of countless lesbians who came out in later life, having previously been married to a man.

I was deeply moved by what Klein had written, which was why I asked her if I could publish it on my Substack. But, to my astonishment, it attracted a lot of negative comments and caused quite a furore. One woman posted:

'I personally don't want a bunch of women play acting same-sex attraction when they are not. I don't want women forcing themselves to have sex with other women. It really is devastating to a lesbian to have a woman pretending and not truly be into her. It's hurtful.'

And another:

'Is it not enabling homophobes to claim that women can choose to be lesbians? This feels very similar to men claiming to be women. It's not that you should *call* yourself bisexual, you ARE bisexual.'

So I was pleased to read a response from the wonderful Liane Timmermann, who wrote:

'I send Sisterhood to all my lesbian sisters, the ones who always knew and the late bloomers #BornThisWayMyArse

'As most of you know, I was always attracted to women and not to men and always considered myself a lesbian, but I am also a lesbian feminist consciously (meaning through consciousness-raising in my early lesbian life). This is because when I was 17 there was a strong feminist movement to join. I grew up in our Women's Liberation Movement and I was actively involved in it.

'I read my first radical feminist book (Mary Daly, Gyn/ecology) then. I consider all this very lucky. Who knows what would have happened to me if I would have not had this. Women-only spaces were the norm. Because I was a lesbian and because of my political activism lots of things happened to me, for example attempted rape, endless attacks verbally and physically. I was shot at, attacked with a knife (still got the scars) and experienced many other acts of hatred against me and my sisters.

'For me being a lesbian also means that I dismantled patriarchy in understanding how it works on women. So for me, it is also political to be a lesbian.

'It breaks my heart to have noticed, especially in the last few years, that so many would rather call themselves bisexual than a lesbian because they had a heterosexual past. I find the idea that you can only be a "real" lesbian if you are a "born lesbian" deeply anti-lesbian and misogynist. Lots of lesbians who came out later have different life experiences. So many of us experienced peer/family pressure and fear. Then came pornography, coercive control, rape, abuse – depending on what kind of fucked up families we were born into which have kept/are still keeping women in heterosexuality.

'On top of everything else they did not have a women's movement, and no women-only spaces. If a woman comes out of heterosexuality, whatever her age or her reason, I welcome her with open arms – and most women actually come out as lesbians through politics because they can see what has been done to them by patriarchy. You can only see when you are actually out of the situation, not when you are still in it.

'Please stop creating a hostile environment for other lesbians who maybe were not consciously lesbians when they were in the womb but became lesbians in later life.

'We are being attacked from every angle as girls, as women, as lesbians. Our rights as females are being stripped away one by one. So get a grip, women – and attack and fight patriarchy.'

It is imperative that we look at how and why the debate has become so polarised in recent years, and question the hostility directed towards any lesbian who dares mention 'choice' or who challenges the notion that we are 'born that way' from a feminist perspective, by which I mean women finding the courage and opportunity to act upon deep-rooted desires rather than be condemned to unhappy heterosexuality for life. I am often called 'bisexual', used as an insult by the 'gold star' lesbians discussed earlier. I find that whole 'gold star' concept alienating, and although it's a club I qualify to join,[3] like Groucho Marx, I would decline. Klein herself is obviously not a believer in the 'gay gene'; the response she gave to the critical comments posted beneath her essay was: 'I can only despair... totally unproven and women- and lesbian-hating. Do your research. Love women because you want to!'

I was asked if I had published Klein's essay because I knew it would cause controversy. Absolutely not. I don't publish articles for clicks. I thought it was a terrific piece of writing and was proud to share it; I suppose I thought (or hoped) it would speak for itself. I also wanted women who somehow managed to avoid compulsory heterosexuality to realise how fortunate they were. As one woman commented: 'The patriarchy does not peddle choice. If women were educated to know they have one, our male dominated system would collapse.'

The feminist pushback against the 'gold star' lesbians' comments was both heart-warming and deeply reassuring. Many were as appalled as Timmermann that a lesbian feminist who has devoted decades to the fight for the liberation of women was being maligned and misrepresented for writing about how proud and happy she is to be a lesbian and sees it not just as an active, positive choice but as the 'best decision' of her life. Some lesbians identified closely with Renate's experience, even if they themselves had never had sex with a man, and recognised that the choice to be a lesbian often comes hand in hand with the discovery of feminism. As my friend Joan Scanlon (she of the Open University Women's Studies summer school) wrote to me when we were discussing the controversy:

'Through feminism I realised that my choice to be a lesbian was a choice about how I identified as a woman, about identifying with other women (instead of gay men), and it all suddenly made sense. Being a lesbian became something to celebrate; instead of being an outsider, a sexual outlaw, I found myself amongst women who were proud of their identity, enjoyed a strong sense of community, and were political activists with agency in the world. I had long identified as a lesbian, never been attracted to men, but feminism was the key to recognising I had more in common with other women, across differences of race and class AND sexuality, than I had in common with men who were same-sex-attracted. It never occurred to me that it was genetic, but if it had, feminism would have put paid to that idea.'

## Fightback

As we have seen, masses of flak is being thrown at lesbians – but we are not taking it lying down. Lesbian involvement with and attendance at FiLiA have been on the rise for several years and we are now an integral part of it. The FiLiA website hosts valuable resources for lesbians, including an authoritative guide for lesbian organisers on defending our spaces, our groups and our lives,[4] and a short guide to lesbian rights to spaces[5] – a project initiated by LGB Alliance Cymru, who worked on the production of these guides with brilliant feminist barrister Naomi Cunningham. It has links with the Lesbian Immigration Support Group, which campaigns to support the lesbian refugees trapped at the Kakuma Refugee Camp in Kenya, as described in Chapter 3. In 2021, some Kakuma women addressed the conference over a live link, which resulted in Joanna Cherry raising the issue in Parliament.[6] FiLiA also runs Labrys Lit, an international lesbian book group – one of the many lesbian-themed workshops and spaces. 'It is so good to walk in [to the annual FiLiA conference] and see more than a hundred lesbians sat in clusters on the floor, holding enthusiastic, animated discussions', one delegate told me. Where feminists gather, lesbians are always to be found, and vice versa. We are recognising that our lives, our struggles, our friendships and our social lives are indivisible.

I became friends with Martina Navratilova, lesbian icon and one of the greatest tennis players of all time, when we started talking about lesbian feminist issues. I had never forgotten watching her play at Wimbledon the year after she came out. It was 1982; I was 20. The backlash against her had been brutal – she once estimated that she lost around US$10 million in endorsement deals as a result. Navratilova was one of the first lesbian role models for my generation; we all felt enormous pride that she was one of our own.

When I interviewed her in 2010 for the *Guardian*, she told me that I was the first out lesbian writing in the national press in any country to do so. We spoke of the sexism that underlay the anti-lesbianism she had fought against throughout her career, and discovered that we had much in common. Navratilova is only too aware of how the conflation of sex with gender affects lesbians, in sport and elsewhere. Before the Glasgow FiLiA conference in 2023 I asked if she would like to send a message to the attendees, and in particular to J. K. Rowling. She made an audio recording which included the line, 'Fuck the patriarchy', and she addressed Rowling directly with the words, 'I fucking love you, Jo.' The room went wild. I was beyond delighted when she agreed to be a patron of The Lesbian Project when it was officially launched.

Our private launch was attended by lesbians, heterosexual women, and even some men. J. K. Rowling, who had by then become a good friend to both Kathleen and I, popped in, as did a couple of supportive MPs. Our first statement was a tongue-in-cheek announcement that we wanted an amicable divorce from gay men. Much as we welcomed their support, we wanted to focus on the issues that affect us specifically as women. Kathleen and I talked a lot about the bullying and harassment we were both facing (along with many other women) at the hands of people, both gay and straight, who insist that we are right-wing homophobic bigots. It was obvious to us that lesbians needed to be disentangled from the acronym.

Kathleen and I make a good team because we are very different characters and had very different experiences of coming out as lesbians. Kathleen came out in her late thirties, having been married to a man and having had children, and I as a teenager without any heterosexual experience as such. We had both expressed similar views about how being lesbians had hugely enhanced our lives and made us extremely happy and fulfilled. And we both felt real dismay at the way young lesbians seemed to be moving away from that proud identity and into labels such as 'queer', or even 'trans men'. Kathleen worked in Brighton – once a gay Mecca, now transgender Tinseltown. In leafy north London I was seeing upper-middle-class, liberal parents embracing the possibility that their kids might come home from their expensive (or even exclusive-catchment-area state-run) schools and announce they were non-binary.

We soon saw that there was very little information in social scientific research about us. We were often put in a category with gay men, and increasingly with so-called 'trans lesbians', irretrievably corrupting the resulting data. We were also being lumped in with bisexual women. Bisexual women face the same discrimination as lesbians when they are in relationships with women, but many of the women included in such research are in long-term relationships with men.

We had a list of questions that we wanted to explore. For example, what funding is available in the charitable sector for lesbian-only advocacy? What about the lesbian experience of motherhood? Health needs? Housing? Relationships, including divorce and separation? Where are the lesbian-only projects, and who has access to them? What about data around happiness, or the workplace? We also wanted to focus on inter-generational differences between lesbians, and how we might play a small part in helping facilitate better communication and mentorship.

Before publicising The Lesbian Project, we did some research on what other, similar groups were out there. Obviously, one key reason for setting up the project was that lesbian voices had been effectively silenced by people claiming that we were asserting our autonomy only because we hated trans people. This was when I realised just how effectively and prolifically lesbian feminists had been organising: there was Lesbian Labour, Get The L Out, Crone Zone, Lancashire Lesbians, Lesbian Strength, Lesbians in Wales, Literally Dyke, Lesbian Laborious, Lesbian Rights Alliance, Positively Lesbian, Scottish Lesbians, Green Lesbians, Lesbian Labyrinth, SuperLadies/Lesbiconic, Dyke Voices and Labyrinth Security. Across the length and breadth of the UK, lesbians were organising at underground meetings and public gatherings. In 2023, the first ever speed-dating event for lesbians (advertised as female-only) was held, L Community[7] announced development of the first female-only lesbian dating app, and Lesbian Collective London had their first lesbian picnic at the Hampstead Heath Ladies' Pond in London. The first Lesbian Visibility march took place in Cardiff in 2024, and Welsh lesbians organised a Lesbian Visibility Week. There was also a lesbian-only Pride march on Lesbian Pride Day, organised by Jenny Watson, a lesbian feminist in her early thirties. And in south-west London is Sapphic Central, a lesbian club run by lesbian supreme Lucy Masoud (whose tale of being booted off a dating app for specifying that she was only interested in dating other females I told in Chapter 4). Masoud switched from putting out actual fires when working for the London Fire Brigade to starting metaphorical ones by setting up a women-only social at which lesbians can have a night free of hassle from the usual suspects.

## Moving forward

As lesbians, we have done ourselves a massive disservice by allowing feminism, crucial to our wellbeing and liberation, to be deprioritised and even dismissed. By celebrating 'lesbian porn', by prioritising quiet couple-ism and conformity, by assimilation and apathy, we have allowed anti-lesbianism to flourish. We need to regroup and make it safe to speak publicly about our sexual identity and our political vision again. Being told we represent a bigoted viewpoint has robbed us of both the ability and the confidence to talk openly about being lesbians and about the prejudice and discrimination that we face. We've gone backwards.

There is also a need for a radical reassertion of our distinct identity as lesbians, while reinforcing the kind of feminism that placed women's sexual autonomy front and centre of our demands, as the revolutionary lesbian Jill Johnston did in *Lesbian Nation*.

Women who refuse to engage with any issue relating to women and girls other than gender ideology frustrate me in the same way as commentators on misogyny do when they focus on Andrew Tate. If it weren't for men's violence towards women and girls, what would it matter if men were identifying as women, and if all facilities were mixed-sex? Were it not for the fact that we all understand male violence to be endemic, happening every single day, and pretty much normalised, females would have no reason to fear the presence of men in such spaces.

When I debated the journalist and author Helen Joyce, whom I like and respect, about whether or not women should ally ourselves with the right wing to challenge gender ideology, I objected to the view that we *have to* make such alliances because, as the metaphor goes, the house is on fire, and our children are inside. Helen didn't use those words, but that was her message. I countered by saying, 'The house has always been on fire, with domestic violence, femicide, sexual abuse of children, rape and so on, and our children are often inside. Where were those women [those who focus exclusively on the trans issue] then?'

I now think this was somewhat unfair. First, many of those women are completely new to any type of women's rights campaigning, and second, many who have taken up arms in the fight against gender ideology as a single issue do have a long history in campaigning to end men's violence. But my central argument remains: the misogyny intrinsic to gender ideology has grown and flourished at the rate it has because of women's subservient position in relation to men, and this is yet another men's rights backlash, even though it is flying a 'progressive' flag.

To fight back effectively, we need a feminist analysis of gender and sexuality. Without feminism, lesbianism would still be seen as a pick-and-mix between genes, pathology and depravity. And without the work that feminists did during the 1970s, lesbianism as we know it today could well not exist, moving straight from Radclyffe Hall (an upper-class lesbian whose novel *The Well of Loneliness*, published in 1928, caused huge controversy) to queerness and transgenderism. In the 1920s, a lesbian was thought of as a man in a woman's body. Look how far we've come! A hundred years later, we are being described as... men in women's bodies. In the five decades that have passed since the publication of *Lesbian Nation*, lesbians have gone from being considered radical sexual outlaws by liberals and progressives, at least superficially, to becoming almost an endangered species. This is what we must work to change.

# Epilogue

## An Ending and a New Beginning

Whenever they want you not to talk about something, this is when you know you need to talk about it. I need to scream it from the rooftops, and I will keep doing it. When they then say, 'You're on the wrong side of history,' I'm like, 'Well, you know, I have yet to be on the wrong side of history.'

Martina Navratilova, in conversation<br>with the author, 2024

For the women that have experienced male violence, finding a lesbian community has been a place of great joy, friends and relationships, but it's also been for a lot of them a place of safety.

Sue Regan, academic researcher, in<br>conversation with the author, 2024

I arrive at Sapphic Central, the monthly lesbian disco run by Lucy Masoud, one of only two in London, at 9.30pm on an August Friday in 2024. In the busy streets surrounding the venue, people spill out of pubs, drinking, smoking and relaxing into the weekend. There are a couple of women sitting by the entrance, having a drink, people-watching. Another couple of women direct me to the male bouncer at the front, whose job it is to search my bag and, I assume, check that I'm not a drunken bloke. Next I go to the desk where there is a request for donations, 'however small', to cover costs. As I walk down the stairs to the bar and dancefloor, I feel enveloped in a friendly atmosphere. There's no one dancing yet, but the DJ is playing classic tunes, and the room is getting busier and noisier.

Up another set of stairs, I find a yard where a few women are smoking and chatting in small groups, or sitting on their own, looking relaxed in their solitude. It's the kind of place where you won't be on your own for long, I muse, as I watch more women arrive and sit down, instantly chatting to whomever they end up next to.

It's a little unfamiliar now, coming to a venue where the organisers' focus is on the imperative of keeping men out, ensuring the women inside are safe, and that the event is exactly what it is meant to be – a welcoming occasion for lesbians. Everything has been thought through to make sure it's safe for women to go alone, and that, whatever your age, background or political persuasion, you will feel fully at home.

I have to remind myself that this is not the early 1980s at the Dock Green pub in Leeds. I feel as though we have come full circle, back to the days where we were having to create such events in the teeth of hostility, and fight for our rights to our own space. We all know *why* we're having to do it all over again – but this time it's a matter of *re*claiming those rights. Perhaps, I think, it's no bad thing that we're having to go through all of this again? It does remind us of the importance of this kind of event, which we had arguably come to take for granted.

# Epilogue

When I talked about all this with Lucy, she observed, 'If you're a woman asserting your boundaries, and saying that you're a lesbian, you will be punished, you will be excluded from online dating, which is now how most people date. I would rather date old school where you would go out to a club, get drunk on cider and end up snogging behind the bike shed. But you can't do that any more. Because there's no more lesbian bars and clubs.'

In setting up Sapphic Central, Masoud was recognising a need to go back to basics and make it possible for lesbians to meet in person. 'When I first moved to London in the late 90s, the city was full of gay and lesbian bars. It was fantastic being a younger lesbian as there were so many amazing club nights and bars. But over the years, lesbian nightlife has virtually disappeared.'

Masoud is right. Of the few venues that have not closed down under the pressure of rising costs and the dominance of online dating, the remaining 'lesbian' events that have survived have been forced to include men who say they are lesbians. In the lead-up to the first Sapphic Central, Masoud's promotional output (which, thanks to a limited budget and security concerns, was mainly word of mouth and Facebook) made it very clear that only the un-penised would be admitted.

That evening at the Sapphic Central event, I meet Kelly, a 48-year-old lesbian from south London. Around 2015, she and some friends turned what had been a monthly meet-up with a few other lesbians into a social group called Shabby She. What began as a small gathering in a pub in Penge quickly turned into a casual, free alternative to central London's LGBTQ+ scene and was soon attracting a regular crowd of around 45 women of all ages from Kent, Brighton, north London and elsewhere.

As a radical feminist, Kelly was entirely familiar with the issues around gender ideology and the threat to women's rights. But she never expected these problems to come to the door of this friendly pub in Penge. Her confidence was misplaced. Trans women arrived at the pub in order to join the group. 'I had to be really on the ball, and I was never relaxed,' Kelly told me. 'I was always worrying about the other women.'

Kelly and her fellow organiser decided they needed to live by their own values, protect their members, and stand up for lesbian spaces by making the group exclusively for biological females – even though they knew they would probably lose their venue by doing so. They went about it strategically, first by reducing their mailing list from nearly 2,000 names to about 800 by removing inactive members, many of whom were men, with the goal of minimising the chances of people kicking off. They then sent around a new, carefully worded policy, explaining that Shabby She was for women only: 'All we ask is that you are a same-sex-attracted biological female, and that you respect this policy and this boundary.' The message they tried to get across was that you didn't have to be gender critical, and that it is fine to have trans women friends, but they were not invited to this event.

Their decision did indeed result in Shabby She losing its original venue. And when they found a new one, trans activists did pressurise the management to shut them down. But this bar's management declined to 'thought police' their patrons, and the group continues to meet there monthly, though they do it more discreetly. 'They know who we are, but... we just don't discuss it. It's just an individual woman booking a big table on the last Friday of every month.' They do hope to eventually reclaim their

# Epilogue

Shabby She identity openly, but for Kelly this is a pragmatic compromise: 'The important thing is that our night wasn't shut down by these arseholes.'

Part of the cost of losing lesbian-only social spaces is the loss of the political connection forged there. It's not just about having a nice time, meeting potential dates or partners and being able to relax among our own, precious as that is; it's also about the development of ideas and the important work we've always done to strive for the liberation of lesbians and all women.

In June 2024, I was enjoying a sunny weekend in Margate with my partner Harriet and our exuberant young dog Ruby when I found myself caught up in the Pride parade. My first instinct was to hide my face. The slogans on placards and T-shirts were heavily slanted towards trans ideology. 'Protect trans kids', 'Stand by your trans', 'Dykes for trans' and 'Trans rights are human rights' were all on display amid the sea of pink and blue trans rights flags. I resisted the urge to run away, and instead bought a multicoloured garland for Ruby from a street vendor before heading to an oyster shack for lunch. But I felt sad that my immediate reaction on seeing the Pride march was nervousness and trepidation. I also felt very conflicted. Surely it should do my heart good to see so many women out on the streets, bold and proud – but then, so many of them seemed to be putting the rights of men ahead of their own. It all made me even more determined that lesbians should continue to grow a new, revitalised movement, and take to the streets in celebration at being out in such a hostile and often dangerous world.

A few months later, in November 2024, I spent two consecutive days at the Supreme Court in London, observing an appeal brought by the feminist campaign group For Women Scotland against the Scottish Ministers, regarding the hotly contested question: what is a woman?

Seriously.

It has become necessary, by this stage, to argue in the highest court of the land that a woman is an adult human female, and that a man – even one in possession of a Gender Recognition Certificate (GRC) and thus entitled to a new, fictitious birth certificate – is not a woman.

The Equality Act 2010 is the piece of law under scrutiny during the case, because in addition to protecting against discrimination based on biological sex, it also deals with other protected characteristics including 'gender reassignment'. Many trans activists, including Stonewall, have argued that this means gender identity supersedes biological sex in law.

Without going into too much technical detail, the Scottish government has argued that sex can be changed by a GRC, while For Women Scotland state that sex is an immutable biological fact.

Following?

Human rights organisation Sex Matters intervened on the For Women Scotland side, alongside three groups known as 'the lesbian intervenors': The Lesbian Project, the LGB Alliance and Scottish Lesbians.

As a Lesbian Project director, I was in court. Seated next to Eileen Gallagher, chair of the LGB Alliance, Joanna Cherry, the lawyer and former MP we met in Chapter 6, and other lesbian friends and colleagues, I took a moment to ponder on how the hell we got here. As the KC acting for the Scottish Ministers was arguing, in front of five of the most senior judges in the land, that

# Epilogue

a man who has a GRC should be legally recognised as a lesbian, and have access to lesbian associations, clubs, dating apps and so on, I recalled how hard we had fought for lesbian social and political spaces back in the 1980s.

My favourite line in the submission states that a lesbian is not 'sexually attracted to a certificate'.[1] There was much to laugh about during the two days, but it was on the whole a surreal experience, as though we were visiting a parallel universe.

Recent research commissioned by The Lesbian Project shows that prejudice and discrimination against lesbians persist.[2] We continue to experience general harassment and bullying, including at work. Lesbians are often subject to 'public objectification, fetishisation and tokenism'. Also, 'lesbians are often associated with both promiscuity and sexually transmitted infections, with implications for prejudice and discrimination in healthcare and linked services.' Some research suggests that lesbians are more likely than heterosexual women to be victims of sexual assault, and the experience of sexual assault is linked to poor mental health and physical health outcomes.

Nevertheless, the lawyer representing the Scottish Ministers, Ruth Crawford KC, denied that obstructing the right of lesbians to assemble without men would create a 'chilling effect'.[3]

Crawford tied herself in knots in her attempt to argue that men can be lesbians. If we win this case, which I'm pretty sure we will, it will be the lesbian issue that did it. Consider the following exchange.

Crawford argued that a man with a GRC would be allowed to join a lesbian association, unless it was based on a philosophical belief, such as a gender critical one, in which case they could exclude him. Except, of course, if the man in question is trans identified *and* believes that sex is immutable, and that women can't become men just because they have a GRC. The judge pointed out that the lesbians wouldn't know whether or not he had one because it contravenes the Equality Act to ask such a person to present it. He could present his birth certificate though, said Crawford.

'They couldn't just associate as lesbians?' asked one of the judges. 'No,' admitted Crawford.

One of the judges asked about physical 'presentation', and what the distinction is between a man that looks like a man, and says he's a lesbian, but doesn't have a GRC, and his counterpart who does have one? 'Well, they could produce the birth certificate,' replied Crawford, 'and I've already indicated the person who has a GRC can request a birth certificate which will show the sex of their acquired gender.'

If a man says he's a woman and is legally a woman, argued Crawford, that doesn't mean that the lesbian to whom he is attracted has lost her ability to define herself as a lesbian. 'We submit that the class of persons to which a person is attracted is determined by reference to the person who holds the protected characteristic of sexual orientation. Where the person becomes the sex of their acquired gender, that logically has the effect from the perspective of the Equality Act of changing the class of persons to whom the person is orientated towards. But that, we submit, would not affect the ability of that person prior to a GRC being issued to invoke direct discrimination protections on the basis of the sexual orientation which they consider themselves and others receive them to hold,' she said.

## Epilogue

'And they may or may not look like a woman or a man?' asked the judge. 'Indeed,' said Crawford, 'but the person without a GRC is not a lesbian because they have not acquired the sex of...' She hesitates, shuffles some papers, and looks almost pleadingly towards the judges: 'I'm very conscious of the time.'

◆

At the 1974 Women's Liberation Movement Conference in Edinburgh, a sixth demand was added to those laid down at previous conferences:[4] 'The right to a self-defined sexuality. An end to discrimination against lesbians.' A seventh and final demand was added at the Birmingham Conference in 1978: 'Freedom for all women from intimidation by the threat or use of violence or sexual coercion regardless of marital status; and an end to the laws, assumptions and institutions which perpetuate male dominance and aggression to women.'

I find it difficult to distinguish between these two demands. And the truth is that the gap between legal rights, equality and liberation for lesbians is huge. The equal rights fought for by Stonewall are fine for gay men but for lesbians will never be enough because we also have to overcome the routine sexism and threats of violence that all women face before we can even discern what equality might look like.

Somehow, we have ended up accepting as sufficient the fact that in many western societies the law allows us to do what heterosexuals can do – marry, be each other's next of kin and raise children together. But it's not, as is demonstrated by the astonishingly swift rise of gender ideology and its undermining of our basic rights. We need to reignite an autonomous lesbian rights movement within the Women's Liberation Movement, and I hope that heterosexual feminists recognise that we are all in this together.

Jill Johnston set the bar high for lesbian activism, and always considered her lesbianism the most militant, in-your-face form of feminism possible. She refused to separate lesbian rights from feminism, and considered lesbians to be the fiercest and most courageous of sexual outlaws. She understood that our oppression offers a crucial insight into the structure of sexism.

Lesbians must loudly protest the fresh wave of invisibility that has been imposed upon us. While it is infuriating that we are having to do this all over again, it is urgently needed.

We need to put a stop to the ways in which the term 'lesbian' has repeatedly been appropriated, misrepresented and reduced to a meaningless word.

We need to build imaginatively on Jill Johnston's powerful legacy to create our utopia *now*. Fighting cases through the courts, fundraising, battling our way through picket lines, begging venues to allow us to hold our meetings in spaces where they would normally cave in to the demands of aggressive men is no way to achieve true freedom. We need to move beyond constantly reacting to the negatives. It is time to seize the initiative. We can see what is at stake and how precarious our rights really are. Lesbian chic, equal marriage, tolerance and acceptance, the emulation of heterosexual family structures – these are not the crucial battles here; we need to map out what a sustainable future for lesbians might look like.

Jill Johnston envisaged a movement in which men played almost no role – a feminism for women who prioritised other

# Epilogue

women and needed the company only of other women. But lesbians weren't the only women invited to the party. 'The split between straight feminists and lesbian feminists was extremely damaging,' she said in 2006, 'and in any future wave will no doubt continue to be damaging to the cause of women's liberation.'[5]

Straight women and lesbians must stand shoulder to shoulder; we must locate the rage and optimism that fuelled both the lesbian liberation and the women's liberation movements of the past. And we must build the feminism of the future with an understanding of the present, alongside a younger generation of lesbians made more resilient and determined by an awareness of our own history.

The very best thing I can imagine ever happening would be to wake up and discover that the battle has been won, and there is nothing left to fight for – a new dawn in which the very notion of 'pride' has been rendered obsolete for ever.

# Notes

## Introduction

1. https://www.advocate.com/voices/proud-to-be-lesbian#rebelltitem1
2. TERF is a slur directed at women speaking up in defence of women-only spaces. It stands for Trans Exclusionary Radical Feminist. It is also a misnomer, since these women's concern is about excluding men, rather than trans-identified people, from these spaces.
3. https://unherd.com/newsroom/qc-compares-lesbians-refusing-sex-with-transwomen-to-apartheid/
4. https://www.theguardian.com/world/2004/jan/31/gender.weekend7
5. https://cdn.prgloo.com/media/034ed60aa6564c1fbdcfb03fd8e6a210.pdf

## 1 What does 'lesbian' mean to me?

1. https://www.baycityrollers.co.uk
2. Rich, Adrienne Cecile (1980). 'Compulsory Heterosexuality and Lesbian Existence'. *Journal of Women's History*, Volume 15, Number 3, Autumn 2003, pp. 11–48. The Johns Hopkins University Press DOI: 10.1353/jowh.2003.0079
3. https://www.theguardian.com/books/2011/may/13/shere-hite-film-feminist-sex
4. https://www.essex.ac.uk/blog/posts/2023/02/02/women-are-more-likely-to-identify-as-bisexual-can-research-into-sexual-arousal-tell-us-why

5 https://juliebindel.substack.com/p/the-joy-of-choosing-to-become-a-lesbian
6 https://www.theguardian.com/commentisfree/2023/mar/12/i-came-out-late-only-to-findlesbians-slipped-back-of-queue
7 https://www.thetimes.com/uk/scotland/article/boys-think-strangling-women-is-sexy-charities-warn-h05xdr8gh
8 https://slate.com/human-interest/2012/01/is-cynthia-nixons-sexuality-really-a-choice.html
9 https://www.tandfonline.com/doi/full/10.1080/09589236.2024.2307602

## 2 What's feminism got to do with it? Why lesbians are central to women's liberation

1 I took this phrase, which I always found hilarious, from an insult by Germaine Greer towards Suzanne Moore during a back-and-forth spat between the two. The exact phrase used by Greer was that Moore had 'her hair bird's-nested all over the place, fuck-me shoes and three fat inches of cleavage'.
2 https://www.vancouverlesbiancollective.com
3 https://www.aljazeera.com/features/2022/3/21/a-letter-to-sarah-who-was-murdered-by-a-serial-killer
4 https://www.jccf.ca/court_cases/yaniv-v-various-waxing-salons-2/
5 https://unherd.com/2024/06/british-feminism-needs-a-history-lesson/
6 A pseudonym.
7 Lamble, Sarah (2024). 'Confronting Complex Alliances: Situating Britain's Gender Critical Politics Within the Wider Transnational Anti-gender Movement'. Published online, 23 May 2024. https://www.tandfonline.com/doi/full/10.1080/10894160.2024.2356496
8 https://www.vogue.com/article/billy-porter-oscars-red-carpet-gown-christian-siriano
9 https://manchesteruniversitypress.co.uk/9781526155801/
10 https://amandakovattana.substack.com/p/questioning-the-queen-of-queer-theory
11 https://www.getthelouk.com/blog/category/research/lesbians-at-ground-zero.html

# Notes

12 Including two women who identified as bisexual.

## 3 Why and how we are hated

1 https://medium.com/@swift2plunder/acknowledging-transphobia-for-lesbians-1a9fed71985
2 Not her real name.
3 Derry, Caroline (2018). 'Lesbianism and Feminist Legislation in 1921: The Age of Consent and "Gross Indecency between Women"'. *History Workshop Journal*, 86 (Autumn) pp. 245–267. https://oro.open.ac.uk/55535/
4 Derry, Caroline (2020). 'Mary/Charles Hamilton: Eighteenth-Century Female Husband Prosecutions'. In: *Lesbianism and the Criminal Law*. Palgrave Macmillan, Cham. https://doi.org/10.1007/978-3-030-35300-1_2
5 Derry, Caroline (2020). 'The "legal" in socio-legal history: *Woods and Pirie* v. *Cumming Gordon*'. *Journal of Law and Society* 49: 778–799. https://doi.org/10.1111/jols.12396
6 https://historyofparliament.com/2020/02/27/lesbians-and-the-law-the-wolfenden-report-and-same-sex-desire-between-women/#:~:text=The%20final%20Report%20made%20recommendations,characterise%20sexual%20acts%20between%20males
7 https://agenciabrasil.ebc.com.br/en/direitos-humanos/noticia/2018-08/lesbians-still-made-invisible-and-plagued-violence-brazil#:~:text=The%20publication%20was%20put%20together,to%20this%20crime%20in%20Brazil
8 https://outrightinternational.org/sites/default/files/2022-10/OutRight_IranLR.pdf
9 A pseudonym.
10 A pseudonym.
11 https://sex-matters.org/wp-content/uploads/2022/12/Retrieved-11-February-2021-Stonewall-A-Vision-for-Change.pdf
12 http://www.clrnn.co.uk/media/1031/clrnn3-deception-report.pdf
13 https://api.parliament.uk/historic-hansard/lords/1921/aug/15/commons-amendment-2

## 4 The trans Trojan horse trots into town

1. https://www.versobooks.com/en-gb/products/898-females
2. A pseudonym.
3. https://www.thepinknews.com/2021/10/25/joint-statement-pinknews-and-julie-bindel/
4. https://unherd.com/2021/11/why-i-sued-pinknews/
5. Joanna Cherry KC is another lesbian who has been on the receiving end of *PinkNews*'s rabid misogyny in recent years, to such an extent that *PinkNews* had to issue a grovelling apology for defaming her.
6. My friend, Stonewall co-founder and gender heretic Simon Fanshawe came up with this observation. I only wish I had.
7. A term no longer considered acceptable in many quarters. Since 2006, 'disorders (or differences) of sex development' (DSD), which is a medical condition, has been increasingly used.
8. The expression in its original meaning was coined in 1990 by American indigenous gay rights activists. As my friend Cherry Smiley, an indigenous Canadian feminist and author, says, 'the idea of fluid or manifold genders was a colonial invention of "white men".'
9. https://juliebindel.substack.com/p/why-do-so-many-girls-in-blackpool
10. https://variety.com/2024/politics/global/david-tennant-kemi-badenoch-lgbt-1236048181/
11. https://www.thelesbianprojectpod.com/p/episode-25-free-interview-with-the
12. https://www.theguardian.com/society/2023/nov/01/kemi-badenoch-claims-stonewall-has-been-taken-over-by-leftist-ideas
13. https://yougov.co.uk/society/articles/45983-what-do-lesbian-gay-bisexual-and-transgender-brito
14. Ruth Hunt became the CEO of Stonewall in 2014, having started there in 2005. During her time there she spearheaded many campaigns including those for equal marriage and the right of lesbians to access fertility treatment. In 2015 Stonewall announced it had become 'trans inclusive'. Hunt resigned from Stonewall in 2019 amid controversy over what some gay and lesbian campaigners described as her promotion of a 'militant' trans agenda. That same year, she was

# Notes

created Baroness Hunt of Bethnal Green in Theresa May's resignation honours.
15 https://www.theguardian.com/sport/2010/apr/15/want-save-lives-martina-navratilova
16 https://www.theguardian.com/uk-news/2015/feb/16/stonewall-start-campaigning-trans-equality
17 http://www.rtaylor.co.uk/formaldehyde-pickled-balls.html
18 https://www.theguardian.com/society/2018/jun/06/aimee-challenor-theresa-may-lgbt-inequality-transgender-green-party
19 https://web.archive.org/web/20140913215906/http://www.stonewall.org.uk/what_we_do/working_with_trans_communities/9984.asp
20 Affectionately referred to in my book *Straight Expectations* as 'the lesbian Rupert Murdoch of the publishing world'.
21 https://x.com/HJoyceGender/status/1819679977236763074
22 In fact, the protesters used both words ('Lesbians' and 'TERFs'). https://x.com/OliLondonTV/status/1817592785907921405
23 https://x.com/UN_Women/status/1711048869637697685?lang=en-GB
24 https://www.asexuality.org/en/topic/230050-uks-first-asexual-rights-initiative-stonewall-partners-with-yasmin-benoit-for-the-ace-project/
25 https://www.stonewall.org.uk/resources/ace-report

## 5 Brothers in arms

1 https://www.spectator.co.uk/article/why-are-lesbians-no-longer-welcome-at-pride/
2 Julie Burchill's column in *Guardian Weekend* magazine ran between January 1998 and December 2003.
3 https://www.petertatchell.net/lgbt_rights/age_of_consent/im-14-im-gay-i-want-a-boyfriend/
4 https://www.independent.co.uk/life-style/is-sexual-orientation-a-choice-9582897.html
5 https://www.theguardian.com/lifeandstyle/2014/jun/10/panel-discussion-born-that-way-gay-gene
6 At least some of these actions (pornography in particular) would, in my view, result in harm against women. This mention is off-topic in this

chapter – but the damage done to women in the production of porn is well documented, and doesn't vanish simply because it's produced by and for lesbians. This is exactly the same power dynamic as informs S&M and other harmful practices.

7  Formerly called the National Council for Civil Liberties, Liberty is a UK-based advocacy group which challenges unjust laws, protects civil liberties and promotes human rights.

8  https://xtramagazine.com/power/activism/roz-kaveney-writer-activist-260077

9  https://wecantconsenttothis.uk

10  https://unherd.com/2021/09/sarah-moss-deserved-better/

11  https://wecantconsenttothis.uk/press

12  https://outrage.org.uk/about/

13  The term 'cottaging' refers to cruising or engaging in casual sex in public toilets. It originates from a Victorian-era use of the word 'cottage' to describe small public toilet blocks in Britain, popular with men looking for a brief sexual encounter.

14  https://www.lesbianavengers.com/chapters/london_england.shtml

15  https://www.nytimes.com/2022/04/12/nyregion/nyc-ivf-same-sex-couple.html

16  https://www.theguardian.com/lifeandstyle/2022/oct/01/how-gay-parenthood-through-surrogacy-became-a-battleground

17  https://lgballiance.org.uk/historic-win-for-lgb-alliance/

# 6 Lesbian activism

1  https://www.lava.nz

2  Inspired by Audre Lorde's famous words, 'I am not free while any woman is unfree, even when her shackles are very different from my own.'

3  Although, as I have explained in previous chapters, I was raped as a teenager, which perhaps excludes me (and countless other lesbians I know) from this accolade.

4  https://www.filia.org.uk/latest-news/2022/10/9/the-defence-of-lesbian-space

## Notes

5 https://static1.squarespace.com/static/5f0869a15c33825a87fd8c48/t/634fdf1b86f45865748a59b4/1666178859325/Lesbian_Spaces_-_short_guide.pdf
6 https://joannacherry.scot/newspaper-columns/2021/help-women-in-nation-priti-patel-parents-left
7 https://lcommunity.co.uk/about/

## Epilogue: An ending and a new beginning

1 Lesbians are, of course, sexually attracted to other women, and not to male bodies, including genitalia, male body mass, shape and smell, so when it comes to dating, whether or not a man has a GRC is totally irrelevant.
2 https://www.thelesbianproject.co.uk/resources
3 https://www.holyrood.com/news/view,supreme-court-judges-retire-to-consider-meaning-of-woman
4 1. Equal pay. 2. Equal educational and job opportunities. 3. Free contraception and abortion on demand. 4. Free 24-hour nurseries. 5. Financial and legal independence.
5 https://glreview.org/article/article-121/

# Acknowledgements

To the lesbian feminists I began to meet when just 17 years old, their love and friendship has sustained me and given me a purpose in life.

To the women in the Vancouver Lesbian Collective, and lesbian activists in Uganda, Australia, Italy, the US and elsewhere in the world that have given me their friendship, time and energy.

It has been such a pleasure to work alongside my friend Kathleen Stock in setting up and running the Lesbian Project. Scripting and recording our weekly podcast is more fun than I ever imagined it could be.

Joan Scanlon provided invaluable inspiration and guidance in tackling the many difficult issues involved in writing a book about lesbians. Having regular conversations with her about the themes contained in this book helped me formulate the ideas that ended up on the pages you have read. Her generosity knows no bounds.

To all the lovely lesbians who were interviewed for this book. I am so grateful to you.

## Lesbians

Thank you to Robert Sharman for his sensitive and helpful copy-edit.

Jane Roffe was a great help throughout the writing of this book, looking over chapters and giving feedback as to sentence structure and grammatical errors.

My agent Rory Scarfe, and publisher Mark Richards for their support and expert guidance, and to Ursula Doyle for expert editing.

Martina Navratilova has long been a lesbian icon to me and countless others. I am indebted to her not only as International Patron of the Lesbian Project, but for the humour we share, and her robust defence of women and girls everywhere.

To Jo Rowling for her friendship and pivotal role in the fight for lesbian liberation. I doubt Jo fully realises how much difference she has made, but we do.

To Harriet Wistrich, who I have loved for over 37 years. Without her my life would have taken a very different path. Harriet has inspired, invigorated, nurtured and protected me. Having to witness and live with the constant attacks on me whilst, at the same time, providing invaluable support cannot have been easy. At the same time, she has gone about her everyday work saving women's lives and holding the State to account. Harriet is a true hero, and I am so incredibly lucky that we are together.

To every single heterosexual person and gay man that have stood up for lesbians – thank you.

For those lesbians that paved the way for future generations to be out and proud, may we continue your legacy.